Wills & Estate Planning

Cavendish
Publishing
Limited

London • Sydney • Portland, Oregon

This book is supported by a Companion Website, created to keep titles in the *Pocket Lawyer* series up to date and to provide enhanced resources for readers.

Key features include:

◆   forms and letters, in a ready-to-use Word format
    Access all the material you need at the click of a button

◆   updates on key developments
    Your book won't become out of date

◆   links to useful websites
    No more fruitless internet searches

www.cavendishpublishing.com/pocketlawyer

Wills & Estate Planning

Mark Fairweather & Rosy Border

Cavendish
Publishing
Limited

London • Sydney • Portland, Oregon

Second edition first published in Great Britain 2004 by
Cavendish Publishing Limited, The Glass House,
Wharton Street, London WC1X 9PX, United Kingdom
Telephone: + 44 (0)20 7278 8000   Facsimile: + 44 (0)20 7278 8080
Email: info@cavendishpublishing.com
Website: www.cavendishpublishing.com

Published in the United States by Cavendish Publishing
c/o International Specialized Book Services,
5824 NE Hassalo Street, Portland,
Oregon 97213-3644, USA

Published in Australia by Cavendish Publishing (Australia) Pty Ltd
45 Beach Street, Coogee, NSW 2034, Australia
Email: info@cavendishpublishing.com.au
Website: www.cavendishpublishing.com.au

The first edition of this title was originally published by The Stationery Office

British Library Cataloguing in Publication Data
Fairweather, Mark
Wills & Estate Planning – 2nd ed – (Pocket lawyer)
1 Wills – Great Britain
I Title II Border, Rosy

346.4'1'054
Library of Congress Cataloguing in Publication Data
Data available

ISBN 1-85941-859-7

1 3 5 7 9 10 8 6 4 2

Printed and bound in Great Britain

Contents

Disclaimer

This book puts *you* in control. This is an excellent thing, but it also makes *you* responsible for using it properly. Few washing machine manufacturers will honour their guarantee if you don't follow their 'instructions for use'. In the same way, we are unable to accept liability for any loss arising from mistakes or misunderstandings on your part. So take time to read this book carefully.

Although this book points you in the right direction, reading one small book will not make you an expert, and there are times when you may need to take advice from professionals. This book is not a definitive statement of the law, although we believe it to be accurate as at 6 April 2004.

The authors and publisher cannot accept liability for any advice or material that becomes obsolete due to subsequent changes in the law after publication, although every effort will be made to show any changes in the law that take place after the publication date on the companion website.

About the authors

Mark Fairweather is a practising solicitor and is one of the founding partners of the legal firm Fairweather Stephenson & Co. He and Rosy Border have written 14 titles together, including five in Cavendish Publishing's *Pocket Lawyer* series. He has two children and lives in Suffolk.

Rosy Border, co-author of this title and series editor of the *Pocket Lawyer* series, has a first class honours degree in French and has worked in publishing, lecturing, journalism and the law. A prolific author and adapter, she stopped counting after 150 titles. Rosy and her husband, John Rabson, live in rural Suffolk and have a grown up family. Rosy enjoys DIY, entertaining and retail therapy in French markets.

Acknowledgments

A glance at 'Useful contacts' will show the many sources we dipped into while writing this book. Thank you, everybody. We would especially like to thank John Rabson, Chartered Engineer, for his IT support and refreshments.

Track changes!

Tax rates and tax allowances change regularly. Most changes are announced by the Chancellor of the Exchequer in the Spring Budget, and then apply for the coming tax year, starting on 6 April. The tax rates and allowances in this book apply to the tax year 2004/05. You can track subsequent changes on the Inland Revenue website www.inlandrevenue.gov.uk.

Any book on wills and estate planning is also vulnerable to changes in tax law and policy. The pace of change is speeding up. The Chancellor can now announce changes twice-yearly: the trailer is the *Pre-Budget Report* in December and the big feature is the Spring Budget. The HM Treasury's website, www.hm-treasury.gov.uk, provides the full script as well as useful press releases on the individual measures.

Future policy changes may therefore affect some of the tax-saving strategies in this book.

Welcome

Welcome to *Pocket Lawyer*. Let's face it, the law is a maze and you are likely to get lost unless you have a map. This book is your map through the part of the maze that deals with making your will.

We put *you* in control

This book empowers you. This is a good thing, but being in control means responsibility as well as power, so please use this book properly. Read it with care and don't be afraid to make notes – we have left wide margins for you to do just that. Take your time – do not skip anything:

o   everything is there for a purpose;

o   if anything were unimportant, we would have left it out.

Think of yourself as a driver using a road map. The map tells you the route, but it is up to you to drive carefully along it.

As with any legal matter, your own common sense will often tell you when you need expert help. In any case, we will alert you to

o   common traps for the unwary;

o   situations when you are in danger of getting out of your depth and need professional advice.

Sometimes we pause to explain something: the origin of a word, perhaps, or why a particular piece of legislation was passed. You do not need to know these things to make use of this book, but we hope you find them interesting.

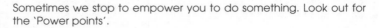

Clear English rules OK

Client to solicitor who has just drafted a contract for him: 'This *can't* be legal – I can understand it!'

Our style is WYSIWYG - what you see is what you get.

Some legal documents have traditionally been written in archaic language, often known as 'law-speak'. This term also extends to the practice of using the names of legal cases as shorthand for legal concepts. This wording has stood the test of time – often several centuries – and has been hallowed by the courts. Some of the words used sound just like everyday language, but beware – it is a kind of specialist shorthand. When we do need to use technical language, we offer clear explanations: see 'Buzzwords', p xiii. These words appear in the text in **bold** so you can check their meaning.

A will needs to make your intentions clear and be able to stand up in a court of law. Why write your will in a 'foreign language' in preference to plain English?

A will is sometimes said to 'speak from death'. In other words, it deals with your circumstances on the day you die, not on the day you make your will. Unless you write your will on your deathbed, the problem this raises is that you have to express your wishes without knowing what the situation will be like when you die. For example, you do not know what you will own, or who you will leave behind, at the time of your death. The art of good will drafting is to achieve precision in the context of this uncertainty. Of course, this is also a good reason to review your will regularly.

A note on gender

This book is unisex. We acknowledge that there are both male and female members of every group and we try to allow for that in the text by using, wherever possible, the generic *they/them* rather than *he/she*, *him/her*, etc.

A note on Scotland

This book is not wholly reliable for jurisdictions other than England and Wales. Scotland has its own legal system. We point out several areas where Scottish law is different (see, for example, pp 1, 3, 14, 22, 23, 26), but if you live in Scotland, or have assets there, you should in any case seek professional advice from a Scottish lawyer.

Get it right – obey the rules!

To be valid, a will must comply with certain formalities about signing and witnessing (see 'How it's done', p 152). As any lawyer will tell you, a defective will can generate more legal fees than no will at all.

Wills on the web

www.cavendishpublishing.com/pocketlawyer

What this book can do for you

This book:

o provides the general information that professional advisers would give you on the subject, if only they had the time, and if only you had the money to pay them;

- o   tells you the buzzwords which are important in this section of the law, and what they mean;
- o   provides plain English wills to meet most needs;
- o   answers some of the most frequently asked questions on the subject;
- o   is supported by a regularly updated website.

If you follow our advice, you should end up with a will which:

- o   does what you want it to do;
- o   is legally sound; and
- o   you as a non-lawyer can understand.

What this book can't do for you

This book does not set out to:

- o   be a legal textbook – we aim to be streetwise rather than academic;
- o   apply in jurisdictions other than in England and Wales;
- o   make up your mind for you;
- o   encourage you to go it alone where there are complications – for example, if a lot of money is involved.

Buzzwords

administrator – the person who winds up your estate if you do not appoint an *executor*. Also, if you die intestate, instead of your executor obtaining a *grant of probate*, your administrator needs *letters of administration*. Where there is no will, the administrator will usually be your next of kin.

Similarly, if you write a will but do not appoint an executor, or the person you want to appoint is unable or unwilling to act for you, the *residuary beneficiary* will usually be able to obtain the letters of administration.

An executor's authority derives from the will, and your executor can therefore take action (for example, to protect your assets) from the day you die. They do not have to wait for a grant of probate. An administrator gains authority from the letters of administration. Until then your estate is, to all intents and purposes, frozen.

asset – anything you own which is of value.

beneficiary – someone who inherits under a will.

bequest – something left in a will (the verb is to *bequeath*; but *gift* and to *give* are usually just as good).

chattel – an item of movable property, as opposed to land or buildings.

Chattel comes from the old French for 'cattle', from the days when your livestock was your fortune – note the link with *pecuniary* (above). Nowadays, chattel mean any kind of movable property rather than 'moovable' in the agricultural sense!

There is also a *statutory* definition of 'personal chattels', which includes cars, jewellery, furniture and other household goods but not cash and investments. This definition applies, for example, where a married person dies without leaving a will. The widow or widower will inherit the personal chattels (see the notes on our *intestacy* diagram on pp 4–5).

codicil – an extra clause added to a will at a later date – a sort of PS and not advisable for amateur will-makers. A fresh will is a lot simpler in these days of word processors.

contingent – where one thing cannot happen unless something else happens first (see, for example, *age-contingent*, p 27. Where a gift is age-contingent, the gift does not absolutely belong to the *beneficiary* until they reach the specified age). See also *contingent liability*, under *liability*, below.

Court of Protection – the court which makes orders for the management of the financial affairs of people who do not have the mental capacity to do this for themselves. The *Public Guardianship Office* (see below) is the executive agency which implements these orders.

Crown or **Treasury** – the Government, who will get everything if you die *intestate* and have no next of kin.

deceased – law-speak for 'dead'.

discretionary trust – a form of *trust* which lets the *trustees* decide who gets what, and when they will get it. Under a discretionary trust, there will be a list of potential *beneficiaries* but none of them will have the right to receive anything unless the trustees make a decision in their favour (for further details, see p 89).

domicile – where you really belong, as opposed to where you happen to be living (your 'place of residence'). Domicile is an important concept in *Inheritance Tax* matters. As long as you are not domiciled in the United Kingdom (or not deemed by the Inland Revenue to be domiciled here) you pay Inheritance Tax only on your *assets* in the UK.

Enduring Power of Attorney – the legal power which you give to someone so that they can handle your financial affairs if you become mentally incapable of doing so.

estate – you might think this means your rolling acres or the family Volvo, but in this context it means everything you leave behind after you die. Your *gross estate* is the value of your *assets*, and your *net estate* is the value of assets less liabilities.

executor – a person appointed in your will to sort out your affairs after you die. (If you do not make a will, the person who sorts out your affairs is called an *administrator*.) Note that your executor(s) will also have the right to 'lawful possession' of your body (see p 113) subject only to the prior claim of the coroner where the cause of death is uncertain or unlawful.

The feminine form of *executor* is *executrix* (plural *executrices*); but, thankfully, executors are unisex nowadays. See also *testator/testatrix*, below.

---

exempt asset – an *asset* which qualifies for exemption from *Inheritance Tax*. The emphasis is on qualifying – there are strict rules relating, for example, to how long you own the asset and what you use it for. Examples can be business assets (see 'business property relief', p 50) and farmland (see 'agricultural property relief', p 51).

GROB – Gift with Reservation of Benefit. This is a gift you make in your lifetime from which you keep back some benefit. A common example is a gift – on paper only – of your home. If you still live in it afterwards and do not pay a market rent, you have given a GROB. A GROB does not escape *Inheritance Tax*, unless the gift is to an exempt *beneficiary* – your husband or wife.

GROT – Gift with Reservation of Title. Another member of the *GROB* family; accountants and lawyers seem to use the two terms interchangeably. 'Title' in this context means ownership.

guardian – the person you nominate to have *parental responsibility* (see below) for your children under the age of 18 if you die *and* their other parent is also dead *or* does not have parental responsibility. Your children's guardian will have the same responsibilities and powers as a parent.

hotchpot – the concept of taking into account unequal lifetime gifts to beneficiaries, typically your children, whom you wish to have equal benefit overall when you die. Example: you have two children, Mandy and Marmaduke. You give Mandy £50,000 when she marries. When you die, worth £150,000, you leave your estate to Mandy and Marmaduke equally, but taking into account (hotchpot) the £50,000 Mandy has already received. Marmaduke will therefore receive £100,000 and Mandy £50,000 if the equal treatment of each child is achieved by a straightforward cash adjustment. But consider whether a cash adjustment will be adequate if, for example, Mandy received her £50,000 30 years ago in the form of a house (which may now be worth £500,000). Hotchpot has been abolished for people who die *intestate.*

Hotchpot (which later became *hotch-potch* or, in the USA, *hodge-podge*) comes from old French *hocher* – to shake, and *pot* – a pot.

Inheritance Tax – a tax, crudely speaking, on dying with what the Inland Revenue considers to be too much money and leaving it (in the Revenue's opinion) to the wrong people. Inheritance Tax is also payable, in some circumstances, on gifts made before your death (*lifetime gifts*).

intestate – without making a will; **intestacy** – the state of being intestate (see pp 3–5 for details).

issue – descendants (that is, children and grandchildren).

jurisdiction – the territory in which a legal system applies. This book deals with the law in England and Wales only.

Jurisdiction – literally law-speak!

legacy – something left in a will; the recipient of a legacy is sometimes called a **legatee** (see also *pecuniary*, below).

liability – (in this context) the opposite of an asset; a legally binding debt. A contingent liability is one that becomes due only if something else happens. For example, if you guarantee someone else's borrowing, your liability is (usually) contingent upon the borrower failing to pay.

Liability comes from the Latin *ligare* – to bind; the same root as *ligament* and *ligature.*

life interest – a situation in which an *asset* will be owned by the *trustees*, but the *beneficiary* will have the use of that asset and/or the income from it for their lifetime.

Life interests are complicated and definitely not a DIY option – take professional advice rather than trying to do something fancy on your own.

lifetime gift – a gift which you make to someone during your lifetime.

living will (also sometimes called an 'advance request' or an 'advance directive') – an advance refusal of medical treatment, but not basic nursing care, which you intend to have effect if and when:

o you lack the physical capacity to communicate your refusal; *or*

o you lack the mental capacity to refuse treatment; *and* in either case

o your quality of life is very poor; *and*

o there is no hope of recovery or even significant improvement.

See p 125 for more details, but if you are seriously considering making a living will, you need *Living Wills and Enduring Powers of Attorney* in the *Pocket Lawyer* series.

mirror wills – wills which come in matching pairs: for example, between husband and wife. A mirror will is not necessarily a *mutual will* (see below).

mutual wills – wills which represent a binding contract between two or more people, by which each says in effect, 'I'll do a deal with you. I agree to make a will like *this* in reliance on your promise to make a will like *that*'. The point of a mutual will is that it cannot be changed without the agreement of the other *testator* – either before or after the death of the first to die. In practice, most mutual wills are *mirror wills*, but it is not necessary for them to be so. Mutual wills can cause problems (for further details, see p 148).

nil rate band – the threshold above which *Inheritance Tax* may be payable on your *estate* when you die, and on gifts that you make in your lifetime except exempt gifts (which never fall into the net), and PETs (*Potentially Exempt Transfers*) which will get caught if you don't live long enough. In the tax year 2004/05, the nil rate band is £263,000.

parental responsibility – the responsibility that by law a parent has for their child and the child's property. This concept was made law by the Children Act 1989.

pecuniary – to do with money, for example, **pecuniary legacy** – a gift of money.

Pecuniary comes from the Latin *pecunia* – money – which in turn comes from *pecus*, which meant a flock or herd in the days when your wealth was in your livestock. Now you can bore people at parties.

personal representative – the generic term for an *administrator* or *executor*.

per stirpes – providing for a gift to pass down in equal shares to the next generation, so that if a *beneficiary* with children dies before the *testator*, the *deceased* beneficiary's children inherit in their place.

Per stirpes comes from the Latin *stirps* – stirpis, a stem or rootstock and, by extension, descendants. As the prophet Isaiah said, 'There shall come forth a rod out of the stem of Jesse and a branch shall grow out of his roots ...'.

PET (Potentially Exempt Transfer) – a gift you make during your lifetime which is exempt from *Inheritance Tax* if you live for seven years after making the gift. All is not lost if you miss the seven-year deadline, because after three years the rate of *Inheritance Tax* payable when you die begins to fall on a sliding scale – this is called 'taper relief' (see p 49). Not all lifetime gifts are PETs. Some are fully exempt from Inheritance Tax even if you die the next day. Others are not even potentially exempt from Inheritance Tax – the main example is the gift of *assets* to a *discretionary trust* (see p 65).

predecease – die before; the opposite of *survive*

probate – the official recognition (technically a court order) after death that the will is valid and confirmation of the *executors'* authority to administer the estate; a **grant of probate** is the document which confirms this.

Read about it in **How To Obtain Probate** at www.courtservice.gov.uk.

Lawyers talk of 'proving a will'. *Probate* comes from the Latin *probare* – to prove or approve, the same root as 'probation', which is of course a period of proving that you are either able to hold down a particular job or, if you have previously been up to no good, that you are a reformed character.

Public Guardianship Office – the executive agency which is responsible for the financial affairs of people who are unable to manage them for themselves (see also *Court of Protection*, above).

real estate – a useful Americanism for land and bricks and mortar.

residue – what is left over after paying off any debts, expenses and *legacies* of money and specific items.

residuary – to do with the *residue* (see above).

revoke – cancel (a previous will); every will should contain a *revocation* clause to establish that it is the last will.

spouse – the unisex word for 'husband or wife'. It's preferable to use this where you are married, because 'partner' is ambiguous and 'husband or wife' is cumbersome.

statutory – laid down by law (statute) passed by parliament, as opposed to 'judge-made' law (case law).

survive – outlive someone; live on after someone has died; **survivor** – a person who has outlived someone; **survivorship** – the state of being a survivor.

testamentary – to do with wills – for example, *testamentary capacity* – the mental capacity to make a will; *testamentary expenses* – the expenses incurred by your executors to carry out your instructions in your will.

testator – a will-maker.

trust – a legal arrangement which imposes a duty on someone – the **trustee** – to own and manage assets for the benefit of someone else – the *beneficiary* (see above) – usually on a long term basis. An *executor* is a form of trustee with specific, short term responsibilities relating to the administration of the dead person's estate.

Pension funds have trustees too – the people who look after the fund on behalf of their pension-holders (who in this context are the *beneficiaries*). Pension fund trustees are, of course, appointed by the financial institution concerned, not the pension-holders.

will – a document in which you say what you wish to happen to your money and property when you die, and who should carry out your wishes. As long as:

o   it is properly signed and witnessed in accordance with the rules, *and*

o   you are of sound mind at the time of signing, *and*

o   you have not been subject to what the law calls 'undue influence' or 'duress',

your will is legally binding when you die, *unless*:

o   you cancel it, or

o   something happens before you die which has the effect of invalidating it (see p 22 for examples).

Even if your will is valid, your wishes as stated in your will might be impossible to carry out for a variety of reasons: a *beneficiary* dies, an *asset* no longer exists, your debts swallow up your assets, or someone to whom you have financial obligations makes a claim (see p 18).

witness – every will needs *two* witnesses (well, one in Scotland). The witnesses watch you sign your will and you then watch them sign your will to confirm they have seen you signing. Note that *beneficiaries* cannot witness a will; if they do, any *gift* to them or to their spouse will be invalid.

Frequently asked questions (FAQs)

Does this book cover Northern Ireland as well as England and Wales?

The general advice is applicable, but Northern Ireland has its own legislation and you would need either to do some reading – try *The Succession Law in Northern Ireland*, by Sheena Grattan – or take professional advice.

Can a letter be as legal as a will?

Yes, in theory. It would, however, need to be signed, dated and witnessed by two independent witnesses. It would also need to be clear and unambiguous. The problem with using a letter is that it is relatively informal and its status as your last will may be in doubt. You'd be better off reading this book carefully, then following our guidance.

I'd like my husband to be my executor, but I'm worried that he might not be able to cope on his own. What can I do?

Make sure your husband has access to good advice. If he is sole executor he does, of course, have full control. If having control will not be important to your husband, appoint a second executor in your will (see p 39) to share the load. Do get their agreement first, however.

If I don't make a will, does everything go to the Crown?

Only if you have no living relatives when you die. The diagram on pp 4–5 shows how the **intestacy** rules work. Making a will is particularly important for people living together outside marriage because, at the time of writing, the intestacy rules take no account of unmarried partners – but see below.

Can I appoint someone who is bankrupt as my executor?

Yes. But might they be tempted to run off with the money?

Suppose I appoint trustees to look after my children's inheritance, and guardians to take parental responsibility for them – how do the two groups interact?

Try to avoid this scenario – it's a lot easier if the guardian has access to the money. If this is inappropriate (for example, the guardian is a loving parent substitute but hopeless with money), the terms of the trust should enable the guardian to have access to funds for the children's maintenance and education.

Can an executor be a beneficiary?

Yes.

How would divorce affect my will?

Under the law of England and Wales, a decree absolute cancels all benefit from the will in favour of your ex-spouse (see p 22). The situation in Scotland is different, however (see p 23).

There is a trap here – if you die between the irretrievable breakdown of the marriage and the decree absolute, your spouse will benefit either under your existing will or under the intestacy rules. It is vital, therefore, to make a new will as soon as you are sure there is no hope for your marriage (see *Marriage* and *Divorce*, p 22, for further details, and for the list of steps you should take in these circumstances).

Does the law treat adopted and illegitimate children the same as legitimate children?

Yes. Furthermore, the intestacy rules and Inheritance Act also protect an unborn child (see p 26).

What happens if my executor dies before me or is sick, living abroad or otherwise unable to act for me?

Provide for a substitute executor in your will – we show you how on p 143.

What if one of my beneficiaries dies before me?

A gift to someone who dies before you will normally lapse. If the gift is a legacy, the money or asset in the gift will fall into the residue of your estate. If the gift is part of the residue, there may be an intestacy of that part of the residue – depending on the wording of your will. It may be appropriate to make a substitutional gift, which is a gift to somebody else in the event of the beneficiary dying before you (we show you how on p 143). There is one exception – if you make a gift to your child or grandchild, who then dies before you, the gift will pass automatically to that person's own children unless you specify otherwise.

What happens if a beneficiary cannot be found?

The executors must first make reasonable efforts to find the missing person, although how far to go will depend on the circumstances and the value of the gift. This may usually involve newspaper advertisements or instructing an enquiry agent. If the beneficiary cannot be found, the safest option for the executors is to obtain a court order authorising distribution on the assumption that the missing beneficiary died before the testator. For small gifts, the executors can dispense with the court order and pass the gift to someone else – provided they promise to return the gift if the missing person turns up.

Obviously, a testator should seek to avoid this situation altogether. One way to do so is for the will to specify the steps which the executors must take to find the beneficiary, such as no more than three letters to the last known address.

What arrangements can I make for my pets to be cared for after my death?

Under the Animals Act 1971, a pet is classed as a domestic animal and is a personal possession. You can therefore leave your pets to someone in your will. Because some pets are costly to keep, you could also leave some money to defray future expenses. Either leave money to the intended recipient of the pet, or set up a trust fund whose income will cover the costs during the pet's lifetime. It seems that a trust for a pet must be limited to a maximum of 21 years (which is tough on tortoises). In practice, do not take someone by surprise with a gift of a pet!

The Will Site, www.thewillsite.co.uk, tells the tale of a lady who left her house to be used to provide for her cat. Sadly, the cat was sunning itself in the drive when it was run over by the hearse.

No, we don't believe it either.

How do I alter or add to my will?

What you *can't* do is cross things out or add things in, or add a PS to an existing will after signing. You can, in theory, add a codicil and get it properly signed and witnessed, but these days it is much simpler and safer to make a new will. Your *last* – this is, *latest* – will is the one that applies.

My partner and I are both male. Can I leave everything to him?

Of course, and we provide a will which does this. In fact, you are wise to make a will in his favour because without one, under the present law, he would get nothing.

Moreover, a same-sex partner is not able to make a claim under the Inheritance (etc) Act (see p 18) unless they are financially dependent on you at the time of your death.

All this is about to change, however: see below.

In 2003, the Government announced measures to end discrimination against same-sex partners (see Watch this space! on p xxii). This should include reform of the Inheritance (etc) Act 1975 so that same-sex partners can claim. In the leading case on the application of the Inheritance (etc) Act 1975 to same-sex partners, Lord Justice Ward stated: 'No distinction can sensibly be drawn between the two couples in terms of love, nurturing, fidelity, durability, emotional and economic interdependence – to mark out some, but by no means all, of the hallmarks of a relationship between a husband and wife.'

Is there a proper legal term for a partner to whom one is not married?

The word *partner* is ambiguous, because it might mean a business associate as well as a cohabitee. There are, of course, many unofficial terms – Rosy favours LILO (Live-In Loved One). If you want to leave something to your partner in your will, name them so there is no doubt who you have in mind.

I wish to make a lot of small gifts of possessions which have sentimental value. Can I do this in a letter instead of in my will?

The answer is 'no', unless you refer to the letter in your will and give your executors the power to hand out the gifts in accordance with your letter. But be careful – the letter itself has no force in law. The safest option is always to make the gifts in the will.

I'd like to leave my car to my nephew. But what if I change my car before I die? And what if I don't have a car at all when I die?

This is a common problem with what are called 'specific legacies'. Remember that your will 'speaks from death'. You can't leave what you don't own. If you do not own the asset at the time of your death, the gift will fail. And if you own more than one car when you die, there will be an argument about who gets which car. And what happens if the car is on hire purchase? For these reasons, a specific legacy of an asset such as a car, which you may change regularly, can be problematic. Consider giving a sum of money instead, otherwise use the *Gift of Mutable Asset* clause on p 142.

I prefer my cats to most people and I want to leave my fortune to the Cats' Protection League. I know my family won't like it and I am afraid that if they get their hands on the will they'll try to stop it. What can I do?

There are three precautions you can take. First, appoint professional executors, such as solicitors, and lodge your will with them. Secondly, appoint the charity as your executor (see p 40). Thirdly, send the charity a copy of your will so they know they should benefit when you die.

The major charities read through all wills that go through probate registries, searching for legacies. Every year they pick up on hundreds of legacies which unscrupulous families would otherwise try to keep for themselves.

Does a will have to be in English to be valid under UK law?

No, but it must still comply with UK law. Just because you write your will in Bengali, Islamic law will not apply!

Do I have to write my will on paper, or would an electronic version do?

No. The electronic version will be insufficient because the law does not yet recognise electronic signatures. As for writing the will on something other than paper, there is a famous case of a will written on the inside of an eggshell which was found to be valid. Don't risk it, however.

Who will own my body after I die?

This question is of more than academic interest in the context of recent scandals concerning the unauthorised removal and retention of body parts by hospitals. Nobody *owns* a body, dead or alive (which means that nobody has the right to sell it for spares). However, the right to 'lawful possession' of the body passes to your executors (see p 115 for a fuller explanation).

Can my family override my decision to donate my organs for transplant, my tissue for research and/or my body for medical teaching?

Yes. The Human Organ Transplants Act 1984 says that your family *may* give permission if you have made a request in writing (or orally in front of two witnesses during your last illness – see 'Deathbed donations', p 125). The same goes for the Human Tissue Act 1961 and the Anatomy Act 1984. Nowhere does the law say that your family *must* give permission, however keen the transplant literature is to persuade you that the decision is yours, all yours. On the other hand, your decision *not* to allow your body to be used for these purposes will be binding on your family.

If you and your family seriously disagree on this matter, and if you feel strongly about donating your organs, tissue or entire body, you could – at least in theory – make compliance with your wishes a condition of inheriting. In that case, take professional advice.

I have a villa in Spain – can I leave it to someone in my will?

No, you cannot give your Spanish villa to anyone in a will made outside Spain. You should take advice from a Spanish lawyer. The likely result is that you will need two wills – one for your assets in the UK and a separate one for the villa. Note also that Spain, like several other countries, has 'forced heirship' laws which restrict your freedom to give what you want to whom you want (see 'Assets abroad', p 14).

If you do find yourself making two wills, take care over how they interact. First, you should specify in each will the assets to which it applies; secondly, you should ensure that the later of your two wills does not cancel the earlier one by an unqualified revocation of all previous wills.

I have been working in the UK on a long term contract, but eventually my employer will want me back home. Can I make a will over here?

The key issue here is what is called 'domicile', that is, the country you call home (as distinct from your 'country of residence', which is where you happen to be living at the time). If you are not domiciled in England and Wales, you should not make a will without taking advice from a lawyer in your home country. If you own real estate over here, you will have to make a will over here even if you need a second will to deal with assets elsewhere.

A foreign domicile has distinct advantages for Inheritance Tax purposes: most people whose domicile is outside the UK (which excludes the Channel Islands and the Isle of Man) escape Inheritance Tax on all of their non-UK assets and some of their UK assets. They may of course get clobbered by the equivalent of Inheritance Tax where they *are* domiciled.

I own a timeshare – a week in Marbella. Can I leave it in my will?

It depends on the legal set-up. The critical distinction is between movable property and immovable property (that is, real estate). A timeshare can fall into either category. In general, movable property can be given in your will, but not immovable property.

Take professional advice from someone with expertise in timeshares within the jurisdiction of your timeshare property (in this instance, Spain).

Even if an annual week in Marbella is exactly what your intended recipient has always wanted, will they be able to afford the flights to get there? Additionally, there is the annual service and maintenance charge to consider. Can your intended beneficiary afford to take on this responsibility? They could, of course, sell the timeshare, but this too would give them trouble and expense.

Discuss your intentions with the proposed recipient first, because a timeshare can be something of a white elephant – see below. A legacy of money might be more acceptable.

If you annoyed the King of Siam he might chop off your head; or, if he really had a down on you, he quietly ruined you by presenting you with a sacred white elephant. You had to accept the gift, you had to look after it, and you could not quietly slaughter it for steaks and elephant hide sofas.

What happens to my debts when I die? Do they die with me?

You should be so lucky! But you can (at a price) take out insurance that will pay off specific debts – such as your mortgage and catalogue debts.

What happens if my partner and I both die at the same time, such as in a car crash?

In practice, simultaneous death is rare. If you and your partner die together in an accident, and it is impossible to determine which of you died first, the law will presume that whichever of you is the elder will have died first.

I am getting a bit forgetful in my old age. Although I want to write a will, and know what I want to do with my estate, I am afraid that certain members of my family will challenge the will on the basis that I have lost my marbles. Help!

Have no fear! Ask your friendly GP to write a note saying that they have examined you and that you have 'testamentary capacity'. Put a copy of the note with your will (and consider disinheriting those who put you to this trouble and expense).

Can my husband and I make a joint will?

No, it is accepted that only an individual's will can be valid. The reason for this seems to be that if you try to write a joint will, the **executors** will have to obtain **probate** for it when the first of you dies. On the second death, there will be no will left to 'prove'. Moreover, it will arguably be impossible to wind up the estate of the first person to die, in accordance with the terms of the joint will, until the second person has also died. But you can make **mirror wills**, which is entirely sensible. Take care, however, not to duplicate gifts which you intend to take effect only once.

Example: You and your spouse wish to give £10,000 to your favourite godson. If you both include a *pecuniary legacy* for this amount in your will, your godson will inherit £20,000. The fix is for you and your spouse each to give £5000, or for a gift of £10,000 which takes effect only when both of you have died.

Can I choose anyone I like to witness my will?

Yes, with the following exclusions:

o   beneficiaries or their spouses or partners;

o   anyone under the age of 18 (16 in Scotland);

o   anyone of unsound mind;

o   anyone who is blind (or how could they see you signing?).

See 'You need witnesses', p 151.

1

Will you, won't you?

Six bad reasons for not making your will

Here are some of the reasons people give for *not* making their will:

1 'I can't make up my mind who's to get what.'

Well, you could always make a will that gives someone else the power to make the decisions after your death. This is called a **discretionary trust**. If you don't make a will at all, your estate will be divided by law according to rules which will take no account of your personal wishes (see **intestate**).

2 'Nobody makes a will at my age.'

Oh yes, they do. Anyone who is over 18 and of sound mind can make a will.

Under the law of England and Wales, 16-year-olds in the armed forces can make valid wills: on the basis, perhaps, that if they're old enough to die for their country, they're old enough to decide who should inherit their assets. And in Scotland, anyone over the age of 12 can make a valid will.

---

3 'They can slug it out among themselves when I'm gone.'

Is that really what you want? Apart from the anger and bitterness, think of the solicitors' bills.

4 'Pull the other one – I haven't anything worth leaving.'

You'd be surprised how much you may be worth, especially when you're dead! In any case, wills aren't just about possessions; for example, they can be used to appoint **guardians** for children.

5 'Her Indoors will get it all anyway.'

It ain't necessarily so, especially if you and Her Indoors aren't legally married! A co-habitee who has lived with you for two years can make a claim, but this is a recipe for expensive, stressful disputes.

6 'I'll do it when I'm not quite so busy.'

And when will that be? Far too many people put off making a will until it is too late. People who die **intestate** – that is, without making a valid will – can leave a time-consuming, heart-breaking, expensive muddle for their families.

And six good reasons *for* making a will

1 By making a will you can make sure your **estate** goes to the right people in the right proportions, thereby avoiding family quarrels and expense.

2 If you and your partner are not married, it is vital to make a will; otherwise your partner, however long you have been together, may get a raw deal. If you are in a same-sex relationship, the law as of today provides no protection at all.

3 If you and your spouse are separated but not divorced (by decree absolute), unless you make a will to the contrary, they may well inherit your **estate**.

4 You can choose your **executors** – the people who will carry out the instructions in your will – for yourself.

5 You can give great pleasure to people dear to you by leaving them keepsakes or small gifts, and you may even be able to right some past wrongs.

6   You may be able to reduce the amount of **Inheritance Tax** payable.

What if you don't make a will?

The flowchart overleaf shows what will happen under the intestacy rules for England and Wales and also Northern Ireland.

Note that the intestacy rules in Scotland are different. We found a helpful explanation on p 15 of the Will Drafters' *Making a Will Guide* – go to www.willdrafters.com and click to request a leaflet by email. Our copy arrived within a few minutes.

Intestacy: how it works

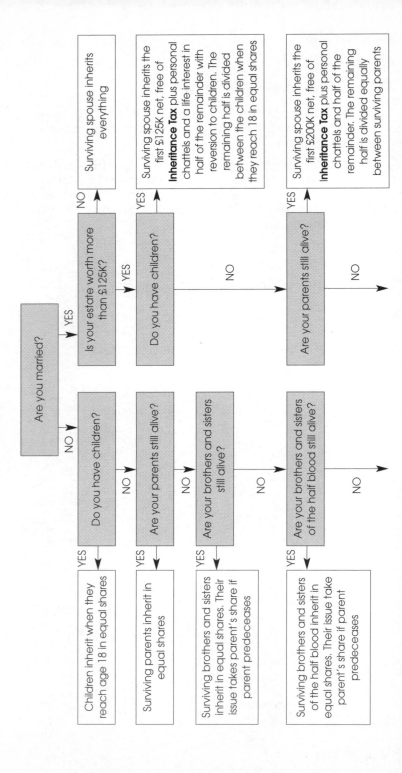

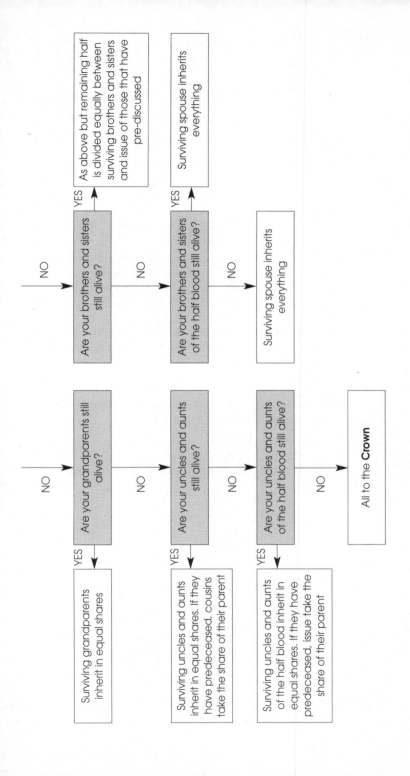

1   Under the **intestacy** rules, 'children' include illegitimate and adopted children but *not* stepchildren.

2   If relatives who would have inherited die before you leaving children, those children will normally inherit equally the share which their parent would have had (this is an example of the *per stirpes* rule – see p xviii).

3   At the time of writing, unmarried and same-sex partners do not get a look-in under the **intestacy** rules as such, but the Government is proposing that 'registered partners' will be able to inherit under the intestacy rules in the same way as spouses (for further details, see 'Equal rights?', p 15).

4   Jointly owned property may pass to the surviving co-owner(s) *instead* of next of kin under the intestacy rules (see pp 4–5 for further advice on jointly owned property). This can, of course, play havoc with the intestacy rules if, for example, someone other than your next of kin (typically your spouse) is the co-owner of substantial **assets**. On the other hand, an unmarried or same-sex partner (whether business colleague or bedfellow) who co-owns property with you might be able to inherit despite the intestacy rules, and from your partner's point of view a good thing too!

5   The widow or widower's fixed sum is payable free of **Inheritance Tax** and costs, and attracts interest from the date of your death until the money is handed over.

2

What have you got to give?

Here are four good reasons for taking stock of what you owe and what you own.

o You can really only give proper consideration to who should get what if you have taken the trouble to work out what you own.

o If there is a significant shortfall between your **liabilities** and your **assets** – in other words, between what you owe and what you own – you may want to consider ways of making up the difference (such as life insurance).

o By calculating your net worth, you can find out whether **Inheritance Tax** is likely to be payable on your estate and, if so, do some forward planning to minimise the amount.

o You can provide your **executors** with a useful summary of what you have and possibly save them time and expense in administering your estate.

Take a second look ...

There can be more to calculating your net worth than just making a list of **assets** and **liabilities**. For example, there may be significant differences between what you are worth in your lifetime and what you will be worth after you die. Consider:

o *Who dies first?* If you have a spouse or partner, the one who dies last may well have twice as much to leave as the first one to die.

- o *Joint property,* that is, property which you co-own with one or more other people. Remember that you only own *your* share (see p 10).
- o *Encumbered property* – that is, property subject to mortgages or other secured loans – you can count only the net value because the bank or building society will want paying back.
- o *Insurance policies in trust* – even if you pay the premiums, the proceeds of the policy will belong to the person named in the policy as **beneficiary** and not to you.

List your assets

Taking into account all these points, use this list to do a stock check of your **assets** – such as:

- ❏ real estate (such as your home, land, etc)
- ❏ contents
- ❏ cars
- ❏ bank and building society deposits
- ❏ Premium Bonds and other forms of national savings
- ❏ other investments, such as shares
- ❏ proceeds of life insurance policies (but see above on insurance policies written in trust)
- ❏ pension and/or death-in-service entitlements
- ❏ works of art and antiques
- ❏ business assets
- ❏ tools and machinery
- ❏ jewellery
- ❏ other *[leave lots of space for musical instruments, boats, radio and computer equipment, racehorses, etc]*

Try to work out the approximate value of what you own.

The total of all these headings will be your **gross estate**.

Now list your liabilities

For example

> ❏ mortgages
> ❏ loans and overdrafts
> ❏ hire purchase
> ❏ credit card debts
> ❏ catalogue debts (money you owe to Huge Universal, Tinywoods and their brethren)
> ❏ other debts
> ❏ 'contingent liabilities' – eg guarantees given for the debts of other people.

Try to work out approximately how much you owe.

Your *net estate* is the difference between what you own and what you owe.

In simple terms:

> ASSETS MINUS LIABILITIES = NET ESTATE

If you have a spouse or partner, you may find it helpful to consider separately the value of your net estate if you die first, and if you die second. It often happens that you get a 'bunching' of **assets** in the estate of the second to die. This means that when the second person dies, the combined value of the two estates may (unless you both do some forward planning) attract **Inheritance Tax** (see Chapter 8 for a fuller discussion).

It's all yours — but can you leave it in your will?

You can give away most types of **asset** in your will, but a few may pose problems. For example:

Jointly owned property

The commonest example is the family home which you own jointly with your spouse or partner. However, the same considerations apply to all jointly owned assets such as shares, bank and building society accounts, house contents and even insurance policies on joint lives.

There are two possibilities if one co-owner dies. The first is that the deceased co-owner's share passes automatically to the other co-owner(s). We call this the rule of survivorship (survival of the fittest?). This is the default outcome when a co-owner dies, unless they do something about it. Where the rule of survivorship applies, you cannot leave your share of the jointly owned asset in your will.

Where the rule of survivorship applies, lawyers say that you own the asset as *joint tenant* with the other owner(s). Where you can leave your share of the asset in your will, you are said to own it as a *tenant in common*. The phrases have nothing to do with paying rent to a landlord and everything to do with the Latin *tenere* – to hold or to own. You will often come across these phrases when you and someone else buy **real estate** together.

What can you do about it? If you do not want the rule of survivorship to apply, see 'Joint property – tying up the loose ends', p 139.

The family home

You can, of course, make a specific gift of the family home, or your share in it, in your will – always assuming that it doesn't pass, when you die, to the other co-owner by the rule of survivorship (see above). But it may not be as simple as you would like it to be. Here are just a few points to consider.

- If there is a mortgage, who pays it off?
- Is the gift to be free of **Inheritance Tax**?
- What happens if you sell the house between making your will and dying, or if you do not even own a house at the time of your death?
- What happens if you own two or more homes when you die?
- What happens if, at the time of your death, you have exchanged contracts to sell the house and/or to buy another house? Which one are you now giving away?
- What happens to the contents of the house?

And if you are thinking of giving your children a share of the home which you own and live in jointly with someone else:

- Can you actually give it in your will, or will your share pass automatically to the surviving co-owner (see above)?
- Will the children be *joint tenants* or *tenants in common* between themselves and with the surviving co-owner?
- Will the children have the right to live there?
- Will the children be able to force the house to be sold?
- And, if the house is sold, will the children be required to use the proceeds of sale to re-house the surviving co-owner?
- Who pays for the repairs and insurance?
- Who pays the Council Tax?
- Will the children be happy to pick up the Capital Gains Tax bill on any profit from sale if, as often happens, it's not their home and as a result they cannot claim 'private residence relief' (for further discussion of Capital Gains Tax and private residence relief, see p 68).

If you are intent on this course of action, please take professional advice. It is often simpler either to:

- include the home in the **residue** of your estate (as long as the intended recipient of the home and the intended recipient of the residue are one and the same);

o   where you own and occupy the property jointly, allow your share to pass to your co-owner by the rule of survivorship (see above).

We would suggest you depart from these rules only if there is good reason to do so.

Rented property

Of course, if you do not own your home, you cannot leave it to anyone in your will.

But, if you are the tenant of a rented home which you share with other people, you should consider ensuring that they have somewhere to live after you die. You may be able to pass on the *tenancy*, although the right to do so is much less available to tenancies granted after 15 January 1989. The precise legal position depends on who is your landlord, and when your tenancy was granted.

The significance of 15 January 1989 is that it is the date when the old Rent Acts went out and the new Housing Act came in. Tenancies granted before 15 January 1989 come under a different set of rules from those granted after that date.

Private sector landlord: tenancy granted before 15 January 1989

The likelihood is that there will be a **statutory** 'right of succession' to the tenancy after your death. If you are the original tenant, your spouse or partner living with you when you die will be entitled to a *new* tenancy on the same statutory basis as your old one. Another member of your family who has lived with you for two years before your death will also be entitled to a new tenancy, although the terms will, particularly regarding rent, be less favourable. There is also a limited right to a second succession. If in doubt, take professional advice.

Private sector landlord: tenancy granted on or after 15 January 1989

There is no statutory succession (unless this tenancy is the successor to one granted before 15 January 1989 – see above). As most residential tenancies granted after that date are assured shorthold tenancies, you are unlikely to have any long term right to stay in the property anyway.

Council tenancy

Unless the accommodation is on a short term, temporary basis, the tenancy will be a 'secure tenancy' that can be 'inherited' by members of your family. If you were the original tenant, your spouse living with you when you die is entitled to 'inherit' the tenancy. Other members of your family, including your (unmarried) partner, may be entitled to 'inherit' the tenancy if they were living with you for 12 months before your death. But there are restrictions. The tenancy cannot be 'inherited' if you are the sole tenant but you were previously a joint tenant, or if you have yourself 'inherited' the tenancy from someone else. If in doubt, speak to someone knowledgeable at your local housing authority.

Housing association: tenancy granted before 15 January 1989

The legal rights of succession are the same as for Council tenants.

Housing association: tenancy granted on or after 15 January 1989

The position of successors is the same as for the tenants of private landlords, except when the housing association has taken over from a council as landlord and has inherited tenancies from them.

In practice, you need to clarify the position with your landlord in your lifetime so that any family living with you will know whether they will have security of tenure after you die. If in doubt, take legal advice.

Assets abroad

If you have **assets** *outside* England and Wales, you may not be able to give them away in a will made *in* England and Wales.

For example, some countries have 'forced heirship' laws which dictate who is allowed to inherit the **assets** which you own in their **jurisdiction**. This applies particularly to **real estate** – your villa in Torremolinos, for example. In Scotland, by contrast, your widow or widower and children have claims over your 'movable property' in Scotland, which can override whatever you say in your will.

You may therefore, if this applies to you, need to make more than one will – that is, one for each jurisdiction where you have assets. In this event, take care over how the two wills interact. First, you should specify in each will the assets to which it applies. Secondly, you should ensure that the later of your two wills does not cancel the earlier one by an unqualified **revocation** of all previous wills (see 'FAQs').

If you think this applies to you, take professional advice – from someone who actually knows about the foreign jurisdiction, which will usually mean an English-speaking lawyer over there. The British Consul in the place concerned can usually provide a list of English-speaking lawyers on their patch.

Insurance policies written in trust

You may be paying into an insurance policy for the benefit of a partner or child. When you die, the proceeds of that policy belong to the person(s) named in it as beneficiaries. So the money is not yours to give away in your will. When you die, the money will go direct to that person.

This type of insurance policy can be a useful tax planning device because the proceeds do not count as part of your **estate**.

Pension and death in service benefits

If you die before you retire, your pension fund may pay a lump sum to your widow or widower. Again, if you are not married you may be able to nominate someone, who may, of course, be your children, your old mum or a partner of either sex, to receive the lump sum. The payment will not form part of your **estate** for tax purposes, as it is **discretionary**. As a lot of money may be involved, it is well worth finding out how much may be available and what you should do to make sure it goes to the right person. Speak to your pension administrator to find out the rules which apply to your pension scheme and what to do to make your wishes known.

Equal rights?

The Government is proposing to improve the legal rights of same-sex partners. The cornerstone is to be a 'civil partnership registration scheme'. Registration will give same-sex couples the same rights (including pension rights) as heterosexual married couples. Pension scheme rules which discriminate against same-sex partners are likely to become unlawful.

Death in service benefit is usually what its name implies – you have to be in employment (though not necessarily at your workplace) when you die. So, if you become terminally ill, take advice from the pension administrator about the implications for your death in service benefit if you were to retire early on health grounds.

Moreover, pension schemes will often automatically pay out a reduced pension for your widow or widower. If you are not married and have a private – as opposed to public service – pension you may be able to nominate a long term partner, including a same-sex partner, to receive the pension instead. The amount of the pension (if any), and its recipient, are at the discretion of the **trustees** of your pension fund, and for that reason will not form part of your estate for tax purposes. The trustees are likely to take account of your wishes. If in doubt, ask the pension administrator.

3

Choosing who will inherit – and what they will get

In deciding who gets what, you may want to treat all your **beneficiaries** equally, or take into account:

o   gifts you have already made (see **hotchpot** and 'Children – a clean slate', p 144);

o   the differing future needs of people close to you.

Typical ways of providing for those you care about are set out in the will forms included in this book and on the website. These are:

o   everything to your partner. This includes husbands, wives and live-in lovers. And Will 1 (see p 158) is suitable for same-sex partners;

o   everything to your children;

o   everything to your partner, but if your partner dies first, everything to your children;

o   everything to your partner, but if your partner dies first, everything to other beneficiaries or charity;

o   everything to charity.

You can also add **legacies** of money or possessions – we show you how.

KISS

The golden rule is - **Keep It Seriously Simple!**

The more complicated your will, the more likely you are to slip up. Some people are tempted to use their wills as a means of controlling their **assets** – and therefore their families – long after death. There are situations where it will be right to protect vulnerable beneficiaries, such as young children and anyone who lacks the mental capacity to manage their own financial affairs. However, if you want to do something fancy, take professional advice.

Mutual wills

Mutual wills represent a binding contract between two or more people, by which each says in effect, 'I'll do a deal with you. I agree to make a will like *this* if you promise to make a will like *that*'. The point of a mutual will is that it cannot be changed or revoked without the agreement of the other **testator**. If you and someone else have already written **mutual wills**, this may well prevent you from leaving your **assets** to whom you want. If you now wish to make a new will, which is different from the mutual will, take professional advice about the extent to which you can do this. You can read more about mutual wills on p 148.

Dependants – especially the ones you'd rather disinherit

There will, of course, be people for whom you very much want to provide in your will, but you must also consider those for whom you would rather *not* provide, but to whom you may have a legal obligation.

The Inheritance (Provision for Family and Dependants) Act 1975 – phew! In future we will shorten it to Inheritance (etc) Act – states that if you die without making reasonable financial provision for your family and dependants, they can make a claim on your **estate**.

'Dependants' for the purposes of the Act *include*:

o your spouse;

o your dependent children;

o a 'child of the family' – that is, a stepchild;

o your ex-spouse, unless they have remarried or a court order has excluded their rights under the Act;

o your (opposite-sex) partner if you have been living together for at least two years before your death;

- any other person who immediately before your death was being maintained by you (this may include a carer).

'Dependants' for the purposes of the Act *exclude*:

- at the time of writing (though this may soon change – see p 15), same-sex partners, however long you have been together – *unless* they fall with in the category of 'any other person who immediately before your death was being maintained by you';

- children of a partner to whom you are not married – *unless* they fall with in the category of 'any other person who immediately before your death was being maintained by you'.

If you want to exclude a dependant from your will, take legal advice. People sometimes want to dodge their **statutory** obligations to a dependant (typically an ex-spouse who has not signed away their rights – see below) and benefit someone else instead. The ploy they try is to make a **lifetime gift** of a large chunk of their **estate** to that 'someone else' – typically their new lover. This ploy does not work unless the giver lives on for six years after making the lifetime gift.

---

1 If you are divorced, or in the process of divorcing, you can get a court order to bar your spouse or ex-spouse from making a claim against your **estate** after you die. This is common practice in an order for financial provision on divorce, especially when the order is made by consent. The concept of such orders is explained more fully in *Divorce and Separation* in the *Pocket Lawyer* series.

  A court order can also be obtained where there is a judicial separation or an annulment. If you believe this may apply to you, take legal advice.

2 If you want to exclude someone from your will who you think would then be able to make an Inheritance Act claim, you should make what is called a 'Section 21 Statement'. That is, you make a written statement, either in or enclosed with your will, that explains your reasons for excluding that person (we provide a sample Section 21 Statement on p 141). A good reason for excluding someone might be that you had already provided for their future during your lifetime. A less worthy reason, but one which often arises, is that the potential claimant would lose out on state benefits if you left them any significant amount of money. In such circumstances, consider a **discretionary trust**.

For technical reasons, Section 21 of the Inheritance (etc) Act was repealed in 1995, but the spirit of Section 21 Statements lives on. If you think there may be a potential claim against your estate, and a Section 21 Statement will help, you can and still should make one.

4

Spouses and partners

If you are married or living with someone, you should give careful consideration to the future of your spouse or partner. Do your best to make sure they've got enough to live on after your death. There can be a dilemma for married couples – how can they make proper provision for the widow or widower on the one hand, and how to minimise **Inheritance Tax** on the other (see Chapter 8, which goes into Inheritance Tax in more detail).

In 2003, the Government announced planned changes in the law which, if they come about, will improve the legal rights of same-sex partners. They will be able to register as Civil Partners in front of a registrar and two witnesses. This document will be like a marriage licence and will entitle same-sex couples to the same rights as heterosexual married couples, including the same treatment for Inheritance Tax purposes.

In June 2003, the DTI's Women and Equality Unit issued a consultation paper, which is available online at www.womenand equalityunit.gov.uk/research/pubn_2003.htm#civilpartnerships.

'Stonewall' have been campaigning for a long time for the law to recognise same-sex couples and you should be able to follow the progress of this legislation by clicking on their website (www.stonewallvote.org.uk/stonewall: click on 'Equal as Partners').

1   If you are wealthy and have a long term opposite-sex partner, you can save **Inheritance Tax** if you marry, because gifts between spouses are tax-exempt.

2   If you are not wealthy and you are the family breadwinner, consider taking out life insurance (see p 85) to protect your family's financial position when you die.

Marriage

Under the law of England and Wales, marriage automatically invalidates (cancels) any will made *before* the marriage, unless the will is clearly made with that marriage in mind. If you wish to make a will with a forthcoming marriage in mind, there is a form of words which will make your intentions clear (you will find it on p 144). Otherwise, make a new will as soon as possible after you marry.

The position in Scotland is different; your old will is *not* automatically invalidated if you get married – but that might make it all the more important to write a new will when you do marry.

In 1837, Parliament was afraid that a man (it was nearly always a man) on his way to the altar might be so preoccupied that he might forget to alter his will, and his bride might then lose out. So the Wills Act 1837 was passed, which provided that marriage revoked any previous will and his widow would inherit.

But if he made a will after the marriage (or before it, with that marriage in mind), the law did not interfere, even if the wife was left out. In 1837 it was considered improper to interfere with a man's right to dispose of his property as he wished. Nowadays, of course, hard-done-by widows and widowers can usually claim under the Inheritance (Provision for Family and Dependants) Act 1975 (see p 18 above).

Divorce

If you get divorced – that is, if the court makes a decree absolute – your former spouse is cut out of your will, both as **beneficiary** and **executor**, but the rest of the will takes effect in the usual way. Remember – unless a court order is in place (see p 19), the ex-spouse may still be able to make a claim under the Inheritance (etc) Act 1975.

Don't Delay! Act Today! Don't wait for the decree absolute. If your marriage breaks down irretrievably (this is the term the law uses):

o   you should immediately make a new will. Don't just cancel or destroy your old will – the **intestacy** rules will work in your estranged spouse's favour. If you die in the interim, your spouse, *who is still legally married to you*, will inherit as if you were still together;

o   *and* if you own property jointly with your estranged spouse, act at once to ensure that the rule of survivorship will no longer apply to your jointly owned property. The law-speak for this action is 'severing the joint tenancy' and we show you how to do it on p 138;

o   *and*, if you are in pensionable employment, consider what should happen to any death in service benefit if you die before you retire. Consult the pension administrator. You may be able to nominate someone other than your estranged spouse to receive the benefit. Otherwise, if it is up to the pension trustees to decide who will benefit, you can write to them explaining the circumstances and expressing your wishes.

Caution: in Scotland divorce does not affect an existing will, which makes it all the more important to make a new will (see below) when you divorce.

Second time around

Consider the situation where you have children from your first marriage and you have now remarried. You will want to make proper financial provision for the children of your first marriage, and also for your new spouse and any children you may have together. Similarly, your new spouse may also have children from a previous relationship. Moreover, these scenarios can, of course, occur outside marriage. There is potential for conflict between the interests of your two families. There is no easy solution unless you have plenty of money. Three possible solutions are:

o   A **life interest** in your **estate** in favour of your new spouse or partner, with anything that is left going to *your* children after your new spouse or partner dies. The problem with this solution is, of course, that your children must wait until the new spouse or partner dies before they can inherit. After your death, there may be conflict between your children and their step-parent. Typically, the step-parent will want to maintain their standard of living, and for that purpose maximise the income from your **estate**, whereas your children will want to preserve as much as possible for themselves.

o **Mutual wills** with your new spouse or partner, by which you leave everything to each other and on the second death what is left is divided among your children *and* your spouse's or partner's children. While we mention this strategy for the sake of completeness, we do not recommend it, because it will restrict the ability of both of you to write a new will in response to changing circumstances.

o You divide your **assets** as best you can. The drawbacks are:

– if there simply isn't enough to go round, either your new spouse or partner or your children might be able to make a claim under the Inheritance (etc) Act (see p 18);

– if the main asset is the family home, it may have to be sold after your death to give your children their share in your estate.

Where you have obligations to more than one family, it is vital that you do make a will: think of the potential claims under the Inheritance (etc) Act. These situations tend to be too specific for a general book like this to offer a definitive solution. Take legal advice about your particular case.

5

Gifts to children and grandchildren in your will

The law assumes that children under 18 cannot be trusted with money, so your executors should not hand money direct to children who are under 18 when you die.

If an executor did hand money over to someone under 18, who then frittered it away on video games, designer trainers and text messaging, the executor could be made personally liable for the wasted money.

Your will should therefore provide a way for your executors either to pay out the money without being held liable for it afterwards, or to look after it until the children are grown up. This can be done in two ways:

o   The will provides for a sensible adult (typically a parent or **guardian**) to give the executors a receipt for the money. The receipt provides proof that the money was handed over in accordance with your will. It therefore protects the executors from any claim in connection with any later misspending of the money.

o   The executors as trustees hold the money in trust until the child reaches 18, or whatever higher age you specify, up to age 25. Any age beyond 25 would normally pose tax problems. You can specify that in the meantime the capital (that is, the original sum you leave) or the income (for example, the interest that capital earns in a savings account) can be used for the child's education or maintenance.

In practice, use the first option for small gifts, and the second option for larger ones.

Points to consider when making wills with children in mind

o   For the purposes of inheritance, the law treats adopted and illegitimate children the same as legitimate children, and unless your will states otherwise, they will all be included in generic references to your children. Furthermore, the **intestacy** rules and the Inheritance (etc) Act also protect an unborn child. However, stepchildren will not be counted as your children for the purposes of inheritance unless your will includes them. Similarly, you will need to make special mention of anyone you treat as your child (such as a foster child) but who is not your child in the eyes of the law.

o   Is it possible that you might have more children before you die? It has always been possible for a child to be born after its father has died, and indeed it is now possible for a child to be conceived after its father's death. Remember as well that both men and women can now have children at advanced ages.

Under Scottish law, your will may be invalidated if you have a child after signing your will and you have not dealt with this possibility in your will.

Wherever you live, leave your options open in your will by referring to 'my children' rather than naming them individually.

o   If you have children under 18, you may want to appoint **guardians** (see Chapter 7).

o   If you have a child with special needs, see Chapter
     6 below.

Age-contingent gifts

The **residuary** gifts to children in our standard wills are
expressed as 'age-**contingent**' – that is, the gift is not
handed over to the child unless and until they live to
that age. In the meantime, the gift is held in **trust**. The
trustees can use the income, and indeed the capital, for
the child's maintenance and education until they hand
the gift over to the child.

There may be a tax penalty to an 'age-contingent' gift,
because trustees pay a higher rate of income tax. This
rate is known as the RAT – Rate Applicable to Trusts –
and is currently 40%, except for dividend income, which
is taxed at 32.5% (2004/05 figures).

Tax is payable on *all* the income from the trust because
trustees cannot take advantage of the child's personal
tax allowance – that is, the annual income the child is
allowed to have – £4,745 in the 2004/05 tax year – before
becoming liable for income tax. You can have it both
ways, however, by giving the income to the child or
using it for the child's benefit, such as to pay school fees,
but the trustees may still find it time-consuming to
recover the tax. This is explained in leaflet IR152,
available on the Inland Revenue's website.

Trusts and taxation of trusts are not a DIY matter – seek professional
advice.

An age-contingent gift begs the question of the age at
which the gift is made over to (or 'vests in') the child.
There are two considerations.

First, there are tax disadvantages if the 'vesting age' is
over 25 because that is the Revenue's cut-off age (see
leaflet IR152: www.inlandrevenue.gov.uk/leaflets/
c5.htm).

Secondly, the law ('the rule against perpetuities') forbids overlong delays before the gift is handed over. This rule affects gifts to grandchildren and what the laws calls 'remoter issue'. In practice, the 'vesting age' for grandchildren should not exceed 21 unless you are *certain* that no more will be born after you die, who could benefit from your gift. This is a complex area of the law. If in doubt, seek professional advice.

An age-contingent gift will generate income (you hope!). This income can be added to the original capital, but this process – 'accumulation' – is not allowed to go on for more than 21 years. Why not?

The rule against accumulation came about as a result of the will of a merchant by the name of Peter Thellusson (1737–97). He was, in Doctor Johnson's words, 'rich beyond the dreams of avarice'. Thellusson directed that the income from his fortune should be added to the capital for the lifetimes of his children, grandchildren and great-grandchildren. The Government of the day did some arithmetic and realised that by the end of this period the Thellusson heirs would own the entire country (this, remember, was before the days of Bill Gates). So they passed the Accumulations Act 1800 to prevent this disaster. Various members of the Thellusson family then spent 60 years arguing in the courts about who should get what.

The dispute was the model for the long-running case of *Jarndyce v Jarndyce* in Dickens's *Bleak House*.

'Class gifts' – including grandchildren

Gifts to a particular group (for example, 'my grandchildren') are known as *class gifts*. There are two common problems with these. The first is to identify who exactly comes into the class. Take, for example, a gift to 'my colleagues at Bloggs's Bacon Factory'. Do you mean people who worked in the factory at the time you made your will, or at the time of your death, and what does 'colleague' really mean? If it is not possible to identify the members of the class the gift will, as the lawyers say, 'fail for uncertainty'.

The second problem is to name a cut-off date after which nobody new can join the club. This is the problem with gifts to grandchildren. How can you predict with complete certainty whether you are going to have grandchildren or, if you already have some, whether any more will be born or adopted in the future? If you write, 'I give £100 to each of my grandchildren', without any cut-off date, your executors will not be able to finalise the administration of your **estate** until the day when no more grandchildren can possibly be born or adopted – that is, after all your own children are dead and their frozen embryos or sperm destroyed!

The usual fix is to restrict the gift to 'all my grandchildren living at the date of my death'.

Lawyers use the Norman French term *en ventre sa mère* (literally 'in their mummy's tummy') for children, grandchildren (and so on) who at a particular time have been conceived but not yet born. A gift to your children or grandchildren includes those who at the time of your death are *en ventre sa mère*.

The legal position of children born using assisted conception techniques is governed by the Human Fertilisation and Embryology Act 1990. For legal purposes, they are usually the children of the people who sought the fertility treatment which resulted in their conception and birth (even if, for example, the biological father is different, or the child has been carried by a surrogate mother under an arrangement allowed by the Act).

Then there is the position of children not yet conceived. Until February 2003, where an embryo was fertilised with the sperm of a man who had died, that man was not in law the father of that child. For legal purposes, the child was fatherless, unless subsequently legitimised or adopted. The deceased father's name could not appear on the child's birth certificate.

The Human Fertilisation and Embryology Act 1990 stated that posthumously conceived children would not have any inheritance or succession rights. The reason for this was to enable the dead man's estate to be wound up within a reasonable time following death, rather than wait, possibly indefinitely, to see what would happen to his frozen sperm and any frozen embryos fertilised with it.

Two determined widows, Diane Blood and Joanne Tarbuck, took their cases to the High Court, where the judge ruled that the law was incompatible with the European Convention on Human Rights (ECHR).

On 1 December 2003, the Human Fertilisation and Embryology (Deceased Fathers) Act came into force. The father of a child conceived after his death can now be named as such on the child's birth certificate. However, this seems to be no more than a symbolic gesture. Registration does not give the child any other legal status or rights.

Special beneficiaries

A note on state benefits

Many people who this chapter applies to will be in receipt of state benefits. Many benefits are means-tested and are not available to people with what the state regards as too much money. Here is the situation at the time of writing for income support/jobseeker's allowance:

○ Adults living at home, where the claimant, and their partner if there is one, are both under 60 years old – the first £3,000 of their savings is ignored. Every additional £250 of savings is assumed to bring in an income of £1 a week ('tariff income'), and this is deducted from their benefits (we wish we knew where we could get such a huge return on our savings!). If they have savings of over £8,000, they will get no income support at all.

○ Adults living at home, with a claimant and/or their partner over 60 years old – the first £6,000 of their savings is ignored. Every additional £250 of savings is assumed to bring in a tariff income of £1 a week which is deducted from their benefits. If they have savings of over £12,000, they will get no income support at all.

○ Adults who live permanently in a residential nursing or care home – the first £10,000 of their savings is ignored. Every additional £250 of savings is assumed to bring in a tariff income of £1 a week which is deducted from their benefits. If they have savings of over £16,000, they will get no income support at all.

You can check that these figures are up to date on the Department of Work and Pensions (formerly Department of Social Security) website on www.dwp.gov.uk.

So a gift to a **beneficiary** who is receiving state benefits may push them over the limit, and not help them at all.

I Beneficiaries with learning difficulties or mental disabilities

If you want to do your best for someone with learning difficulties or a mental disability, it may well be inappropriate to leave them money outright. A person who lacks the mental capacity to handle money cannot give a receipt to your **executors** and, unless other arrangements are made, the money must be paid to someone appointed by the **Public Guardianship Office** as receiver.

Discretionary trusts

The usual way of providing for someone who is unable to manage money unaided, or who may be careless with money, is to set up what is called a **discretionary trust**. This is an arrangement by which the **beneficiary** has no right to the money, but the **trustees** can use the money, or the income from the money, for his or her benefit. In practice, this enables the trustees to provide the beneficiary with extras and treats. Only actual payments to the beneficiary would affect their entitlement to state benefits.

The trust will last for the lifetime of the beneficiary, and you should specify who should get any money that is left over when the beneficiary dies.

For significant amounts of money, there are Capital Gains Tax and Inheritance Tax advantages for trusts which comply with strict rules (although, sadly, the two sets of rules appear to be incompatible, so that it may not be possible to obtain advantageous treatment for both taxes). For further discussion, see the preamble to Will 7.

Choosing the trustees

You need to think carefully about who the trustees should be. Remember that professional trustees will want to charge for their services.

If the **beneficiary** is looked after by a charity, there are other solutions available. These include:

o leaving the money to the trustees of that charity, although you will want to be satisfied that the arrangement will in fact help your beneficiary;

o using the services of the Trust Department of the Charities Aid Foundation (see 'Useful contacts'), which acts as an intermediary, with significant tax advantages;

o in the case of a mentally handicapped beneficiary, appointing the Mencap Trust Company Limited (see 'Useful contacts'). But note that the company will not act as an executor or with family members as trustees, and only administers trusts set up in its standard form;

o in the case of a beneficiary with schizophrenia, using the similar scheme offered by the National Schizophrenia Fellowship (NSF) (see 'Useful contacts');

o setting up a charitable trust account administered by the Charities Aid Foundation (CAF). This confers the tax advantages which charities enjoy, and ensures continuity of trustees. The money cannot be spent directly on the beneficiary, but CAF undertakes to ensure that the money is passed to whichever charity is involved in the beneficiary's care, to use for their welfare. For further details, contact CAF (see 'Useful contacts').

MIND, the mental health charity, offers a free booklet called *Making Provision: Planning Your Loved One's Financial Future*. The booklet won a 'Plain English' award. Its author, Gordan Ashton, is a Master of the Court of Protection. He has a mentally disabled son and in the leaflet he explains clearly the kinds of trust that are available. Go to www.mind.org.uk and type 'making provision' in the search box. From there you can download a free copy of *Making Provision*.

Coincidentally, the most informative learned text on this subject is also by Gordan Ashton. It appears in Butterworth's *Wills, Probate and Administration Service* – a very expensive book, but your local public library may have a copy.

You may not find it easy to relate our general guidance to your individual circumstances, and the model discretionary trust in Will 7 may not meet your precise needs. Don't feel inadequate if you realise you need professional advice – but make sure you consult someone with specialist knowledge. You can find a list of solicitors with specialist knowledge on the Mencap website.

If you think you want to make a gift to CAF, consider doing it during your lifetime. You can then take advantage of the gift aid legislation which adds the basic rate of tax to the amount that the charity gets (see 'Gift aid – a present from the taxman', p 37).

Wills *by* mentally incapable people

In general, it takes mental capacity ('testamentary capacity') to make a valid will – which means that the testator must understand what they are doing, roughly how much they own and who ought to benefit from their will.

People who do not have mental capacity to make a will are not, however, helpless: the **Court of Protection** can do it for them. If you have read up to this point, you have the necessary mental capacity to make your will, but you may know someone who could benefit from this procedure. Indeed, if you are making a will that will benefit someone who lacks mental capacity, you may put them in a position where it would be wise for *them* to make a will.

2 Bankrupt and irresponsible beneficiaries

If you leave money to someone who is bankrupt or under threat of bankruptcy, your legacy will go towards paying off their debts and your intended beneficiary will get nothing (unless, of course, the legacy is enough to pay off all their debts and still leave something over). The same may apply to an intended beneficiary who has entered into an Individual Voluntary Arrangement (IVA), a form of private bankruptcy, where the rules of the IVA often include what are known as 'windfall' provisions to harvest any legacies or lottery wins.

The classic solution is what is called a 'protective trust'. This gives the **beneficiary** the right to income for life, but in the event of bankruptcy, the right to income is replaced by a **discretionary trust**.

Care is needed in the drafting of a protective trust and realistically, if you face this problem you should take professional advice. There may, however, be other simpler solutions, for example leaving money to the bankrupt's spouse, partner or children.

1   If there is a financial black sheep in your family:

    o   if you have already written a will in their favour, make a new one;

    o   if you have not written a will and they may inherit under the **intestacy** rules, make a will bypassing them or setting up a discretionary trust (see Chapter 12);

    o   under the Enterprise Act 2002, bankrupts can be discharged in as little as 12 months (unless the bankrupt did something really dodgy). Find out how long the bankruptcy will run, as you may want to make another new will when the bankruptcy ends and your gift will be safe from creditors.

2   For beneficiaries who are irresponsible with money, but are unlikely to become bankrupt, the right to income but not capital (that is, a life interest in the money) may be the solution. Again, you may wish to seek professional advice.

3 Charities

Gifts to charities are free of Inheritance Tax – and below we show you how to make the taxman add to the gift (see 'Gift aid –a present from the taxman', opposite).

If you plan to leave something to a charity, do make sure you get the name of the charity right. Many charities have names which are confusingly similar. For example, it would be easy to confuse Child*line* with Child*link*. Both exist. Some charities even change their names altogether. What was once the Spastics Society is now SCOPE.

Fortunately, leaving money to a charity, even one which changes its name twice yearly, is not as difficult as it sounds, because all registered charities, like cars, have registration numbers. Your gift will reach its intended destination if you include the charity number to avoid confusion. For example, MENCAP (the Royal Society for Mentally Handicapped Children and Adults), is registered charity no 222377.

At the last count, there were more than 186,000 registered charities, and not all charities are registered (the main 'outsiders' are small charities whose annual income does not exceed £1,000). A full list of registered charities is maintained by the Charity Commissioners and you can search online at www.charity-commission.gov.uk to ensure that you have the right name, number and address for your chosen charity.

The *Charities Digest* lists only the main national and regional charities (see 'Useful contacts'). Lists of local charities should be maintained by local authorities.

The wording of a gift to charity should cover the situation where the charity changes its name or amalgamates with another one, or even ceases to exist. Our charity clause provides for this (see p 65).

Many charities have a preferred form of wording for gifts to them in your will. Call your chosen charity's legacy officer for advice.

Note that some charities will agree to act as your executor as long as you make them a substantial gift.

There are potential Inheritance Tax complications if you divide the **residue** of your estate between charities on the one hand, and non-exempt **beneficiaries** (such as your children and friends) on the other (see the preamble to Will 4 for further details).

Gift aid – a present from the taxman

The trick is to make use of the income tax relief known as 'gift aid'. Instead of making the gift to charity in your will, you should try to do it during your lifetime. The effect of the gift aid legislation is to add the basic rate of tax to the amount that the charity gets – and you can set the gift against any high rate tax for which you may otherwise be liable.

If you want to make the gift in your will, you can still take advantage of the gift aid scheme by leaving the money to a *trusted* relation or friend (that is, one who will not pocket the money!) with a request for them to pass the money on to your chosen charity. The gift will still qualify for the Inheritance Tax exemption on your death, and the taxman treats the onward gift by your representative as net of income tax. The charity reclaims at the basic rate of tax, and your representative can claim at the higher rate. (The scheme, of course, fails in its objective if your trusted relation or friend dies before you, so include a substitutional gift to the charity direct.)

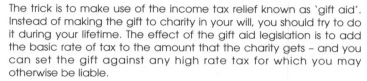

4 Clubs and societies

You may want to make a gift to your favourite club or society. Some of the same considerations apply as with gifts to charity. You need to be sure of the correct name of the organisation, and make provision for what will happen if it changes its name, amalgamates with another organisation or even closes down before you die. Again, check with the organisation before you make the gift and ask them for the wording they would like you to use in your will.

It is also worthwhile finding out whether the organisation is itself a charity. Many are not, but it is not unusual for them to have links with charitable trusts and the tax breaks (see above) that go with them. If this applies to your chosen organisation, make the gift to the charitable trust rather than the organisation itself to protect your gift from the taxman.

Gifts to community amateur sports clubs ('CASCs')

Since 2002, an *amateur* sports club has been able to choose between becoming a registered charity and applying to the Inland Revenue for CASC status.

CASCs must be:

o   open to the whole community; *and*
o   strictly for amateurs; *and*
o   promote a nationally recognised, healthy sport (presumably bar billiards is out!).

Gifts to CASCs, either in your lifetime or in your will, are exempt from **Inheritance Tax** – but don't assume your local darts club is a CASC or, indeed, a charity. Check before making the gift or writing your will. More about this on www.inlandrevenue.gov.uk/budget2004.

7

Appointing executors and guardians

Your **executors** will sort out your affairs after your death, but who should you choose? Bear in mind that your executors will be in a position of responsibility. An executor has a duty to exercise reasonable skill and care. They also have a **statutory** duty of care in carrying out certain functions, such as:

○ making investments;

○ arranging insurance;

○ delegating tasks.

An executor who causes financial loss to your **estate** through failure to exercise skill and care can be sued by your **beneficiaries**. You can write your will to modify or exclude these statutory duties. If you intend to appoint a family member as executor, you may wish to protect them in this way. On the other hand, where you appoint a professional executor, such as a solicitor, you have a right to expect them to exercise a higher level of skill and care than a lay executor – and if they get it wrong, they should be liable for the consequences.

Your executors' responsibilities are practical as well as financial. They will have the right to 'lawful possession' of your body after your death, subject only to the prior claim of the coroner if the cause of your death is uncertain or unlawful. This gives your executors the final say (whatever wishes you have expressed in your will) in the disposal of your body, and that includes confirming or withholding consent for organ, tissue or whole-body donation.

Here, first, is a list of people you should *not* appoint:

o   people under the age of 18;

o   people who will not be able to cope – although bear in mind that they can, of course, get professional help (at a price);

o   people you do not trust;

o   people who live too far away or are too busy.

A useful mnemonic when appointing executors is **TACO** – **T**rustworthy – **A**ccessible – **C**ompetent – **O**ver 18.

You do not *need* to appoint a professional executor, such as a solicitor or a bank (although they may seek to convince you that you should), but it may be sensible to do so if there is no one in your family willing or able to take on the duty of care – see above. There may be compelling reasons to appoint a professional if:

o   the family would otherwise be at each other's throats;

o   your affairs are complicated;

o   the terms of your will impose long term responsibilities on your executors/trustees.

But beware – the professionals won't do it for free and once you are dead they are difficult to get rid of. Banks tend to be more expensive than solicitors – try to get an indication of what they will charge.

Charities as executors

If you intend to leave a reasonable amount to a charity, you may be able to appoint the charity, or an officer of the charity, as your executor. If the charity itself is to act as executor, it must be what is known as a 'Trust Corporation', which gives it the legal standing to take out grants of probate. Otherwise, the charity can still in effect act, but the grant of **probate** will be taken out by an officer of the charity, such as the Finance Director. Before appointing a charity as your executor, ask:

o   is this something they would like to do? If the potential gift is substantial they may well be pleased to do so, if only to protect their share of your **estate**.

o   What wording do they want you to use? In particular, will you be appointing the charity itself or one of its officers?

o   What charges will be made for this service? The charity itself will probably not be allowed to charge you, but they may want to pass on solicitors' costs. Some charities, however, have an in-house executorship service which will do the legal work, possibly without charge to your estate.

You can find out more in a helpful leaflet, *Leave the World a Better Place*. It is available on the web at www.rememberacharity.org.uk – more details in 'Useful contacts'.

How many executors?

You can appoint as many executors as you like, but only the first four will be allowed to take out the grant of **probate**, that is to say, obtain official permission to administer your estate after you die.

Although this is something of a rarity, you can have additional executors for particular **assets**; for example, an author might appoint a literary executor to protect their intellectual property rights on the books they have had published. Similar considerations would apply to artists, musicians, software designers and other creative people whose High Street solicitor and/or family might not have expert knowledge of their field or how to realise the value of their **estate**.

If everything is going to your spouse or partner, it may be sensible to make them your sole executor. Otherwise, two is usually the ideal number of executors. One executor can keep an eye on the other and they can help each other. You will often need two executors anyway to deal with any **real estate**, because there are technical rules which prevent sole **trustees** from selling property in certain circumstances. The most frequent example is where the trustee is the surviving co-owner of property owned as 'tenants in common' (see p 10 for an explanation).

Consider appointing a substitute executor – like an understudy in the theatre – who can take the place of someone who when you die is unable or unwilling to act.

When is an executor not an executor? When they're a trustee.

Your executors will administer your estate – obtain the grant of probate, collect together your assets, convert them into money where appropriate, pay debts, bills and taxes, distribute legacies and the residue and generally sort everything out in the short term. Your executors will conclude their work by:

o   producing what is known as an estate account, showing what your assets and liabilities were and what has been done with them; and (if applicable)

o   signing the paperwork to put assets into the names of the beneficiaries, or whoever will hold them in the long term.

Where there are long term considerations, such as managing a trust fund for your children under 18, the executors will either hand over to trustees or – more commonly – they themselves will become trustees: the same people wearing different hats. Some of our wills provide for this change of role; see in particular the wills that make residuary gifts to children who may be under 18 when you die, and Will 7, which sets up a discretionary trust for a mentally disabled child of any age.

Don't give someone a nasty shock when you die! If you want to appoint someone as your executor, ask them first (although legally you don't need to do so). Here is a sample letter asking someone to be your executor.

Dear

I shall shortly be making my Will and I should very much like to name you as one of my executors, together with *[name]*. You and *[name]* would be responsible for carrying out the instructions in my Will. You would have a duty to exercise reasonable skill and care in doing so. Your out-of-pocket expenses would of course be paid, but you would not be paid for your time.

Could you please let me know if you are willing to take this on?

Yours ever

Guardians

Victorian novels feature orphans and the guardians who had total control over their lives. The guardian took on the powers and responsibilities of the child's dead parents.

The basic function of a guardian remains the same today, but the legal framework has evolved and is now on a **statutory** basis under the Children Act 1989. Under the Act, the child's interests are paramount.

What does a guardian do?

A guardian takes on **parental responsibility** for a child and cares for the child when there is no parent to do so. This is why forms giving written permission for a child to go on a school trip or to have an operation have to be signed by a 'Parent or Guardian'.

Who can appoint a guardian?

A parent with parental responsibility for a child under 18 (including an adopted or illegitimate child) may appoint a guardian for that child.

o   The *mother* of a child automatically has parental responsibility, irrespective of marital status.

- The *father* will have automatic parental responsibility *if he was married to the mother at the time of the child's birth*.
- But otherwise the father will not normally have parental responsibility unless he applies to a court for it or the mother grants it using the official form.

You can find out more about parental responsibility in *Divorce and Separation* in the *Pocket Lawyer* series.

A guardian may also be appointed by the court, in which case the child becomes a ward of court.

'Guard/guardian', 'warden' and 'ward' all come from the same old Germanic root word. In old French, this root evolved into *garde/gardien*, etc. English kept the 'ward' words but later also borrowed 'guard' and 'guardian' from the (later) French. So a warden and a guardian have the same role.

When does the appointment of a guardian take effect?

The guardian will take over after you die, if the other parent is also dead. The guardian can also take over if the other parent is still alive when you die, provided *either*:

- at that time, the child has been living with the guardian under a residence order (which is an order from the court that the child should live with them. More about residence orders in *Divorce and Separation* in this series); *or*
- the other parent does not have **parental responsibility**.

How is a guardian appointed?

In practice, it is convenient to do this in your will (see Will 2, p 160). In theory, it can also be done in a separate document as long as it is signed in the presence of two **witnesses** (one in Scotland), and dated.

Appointing guardians is particularly important to unmarried mothers because the child's father does not automatically have parental responsibility (see above).

Ask before you appoint!

Your children's guardian will have **parental responsibility** for them until the children reach 18. This can place a big personal and financial burden on the guardian, so you need to make sure the potential guardian agrees in advance to take it on.

Finance for guardians

You should, if possible, leave some money in your will for your children's needs, and/or consider buying yourself some life insurance cover.

But there is help on offer. Broadly speaking, in handing out benefits and making tax allowances, government departments make little distinction between a child in the care of a guardian and the guardian's own children.

Child benefit: if the child lives with the guardian, the guardian will qualify for the ordinary, non-means-tested child benefit, just as a natural parent would. The rates as of 12 April 2004 are £16.50 per week for the first child (£17.55 if the parent is a lone parent), and £11.05 for the second child and subsequent children. They can get a claim pack by calling 0845 302 1444 or download one from:
www.dwp.gov.uk/lifeevent/benefits/child_benefit.asp.

Guardian's allowance: this is a non-means-tested weekly payment which guardians can claim in addition to child benefit. As of 2004, the weekly rate is £11.85. To get a claim pack, the guardian needs to call the Guardian's Allowance Unit on 0845 302 1464. Alternatively, they can download a Guardian's Allowance booklet and form. Go to:
www.dwp.gov.uk/lifeevent/benefits/guardians_allowance.asp.

Income support/family tax credit: guardians receiving either of these means-tested benefits can claim for the children in their care just as a natural parent would.

Tax relief: a guardian can also claim the usual allowances against income tax. Your local Inland Revenue office will advise on your individual case.

Child maintenance will usually continue after your death and be passed on to the child's guardian. Any court order for child maintenance will remain in force and the money will be paid to the guardian for the child's benefit. If an absent parent is paying child support through the Child Support Agency at the time of your death, the order will lapse, *but* the guardian can immediately make a fresh claim as if they were the parent. They should call the Child Support Agency National Helpline on 08457 133 133. For background information, click on www.csa.gov.uk.

8

Inheritance Tax 1 – all about Inheritance Tax

You may think that only spectacularly rich people need to read this chapter, but Inheritance Tax is more of a problem for people of modest wealth whose tax avoidance options, by comparison to the really affluent, are limited. All the same, people of modest wealth are in fact in a minority. The Inland Revenue certainly want you to think so. Their leaflet *Inheritance Tax – An Introduction* (see www.inlandrevenue.gov.uk) says cheerfully, 'Here's the good news. More than 96% of estates do not have to pay any inheritance tax, because they are below the threshold'.

The threshold they are talking about is the **nil rate band**, which in the tax year 2004/05 is £263,000. Above the nil rate band, the rate of Inheritance Tax on death is 40%.

Nil rate band? Think of a garden wall with climbing plants growing up it. The top of the wall marks the nil rate band. Any foliage that pokes its head over the top of the wall is liable to be drastically pruned – by two-fifths, to be precise – by the Revenue.

High property prices mean that quite a modest family home in a desirable location can be worth more than the nil rate band, and therefore potentially liable to attract Inheritance Tax, quite apart from any other **assets** you might have. As a result, an increasing number of **estates** are liable to be caught in the Inheritance Tax net.

There is an important distinction to make between tax *avoidance* – that is, tax planning – which is legal, and tax *evasion*, which is not legal. Your will can be a tax planning tool, although it is not the only one in the toolkit. For effective tax planning, you need to understand the exemptions and reliefs and then work out ways of applying them to your advantage. This chapter shows you how.

What is Inheritance Tax a tax *on*?

Inheritance Tax is a misleading name. It is *not* a tax on inheriting. In general terms, Inheritance Tax is a tax on dying with what the Inland Revenue classes as too much money, after:

- adding back any **lifetime gifts** which are not exempt from Inheritance Tax or have not timed out (see p 56);
- taking out 'exempt assets' (see p 50 for an explanation); and
- taking out gifts to 'exempt beneficiaries' (see p 55).

Inheritance Tax, if any is due, is charged on the part of your net **estate**, after making the necessary adjustments (see above), that exceeds the **nil rate band**.

For Inheritance Tax purposes, your estate embraces all your **assets** worldwide and can include:

- assets you own in your name;
- your share of assets you own jointly with someone else;
- gifts from which you keep back some benefit, such as a house you still live in and for which you do not pay a market rent, although you have given it to someone else (known to lawyers and accountants as '**GROBs: Gifts with Reservation of Benefit**');
- assets held in **trust** from which you get some personal benefit, such as an income;
- the value of insurance policies (except 'policies written in trust' (see p 14); and
- the value of gifts that you make in the seven years before you die, *except* exempt gifts (see below), although 'taper relief' on **potentially exempt transfers (PETs)** may reduce the tax burden if you do not stay the full distance of seven years, but live for three years or more after making the gift.

As we said, in the tax year 2004/05 the nil rate band is £263,000.

The rate of Inheritance Tax on death is currently 40%.

So, if the net value of your estate is £262,999 (or less), there is no Inheritance Tax to pay.

If the net value of your estate is £273,000, however, there will be tax to pay at 40% on £10,000 – that is, Inheritance Tax of £4,000 on the part of your estate which comes above the nil rate band line.

Here's an example where a **potentially exempt transfer (PET)** is added back because it did not time out (seven years, remember) and taper relief had not kicked in (which it does after three years).

Net Value of Estate:	£273,000	
Add PET of	£50,000	made two years before death
Total Taxable Amount:	£323,000	
Minus	£263,000	nil rate band
Amount exceeding nil rate band:	£60,000	
40% of £60,000 =	£24,000	
Inheritance Tax payable =	£24,000	

When does Inheritance Tax *not* apply?

Know your enemy. The taxman grants certain exemptions and reliefs from Inheritance Tax. An understanding of these exemptions and reliefs is the key to minimising the tax payable on your **estate** after your death. Not all of these exemptions and reliefs are readily available to most people, however, as you will see shortly. You need to pick and mix the ones that fit *your* circumstances (think of it as a bag of liquorice allsorts!).

Exempt assets

1 Business assets

For a private individual, anything above the **nil rate band** is potentially fair game for the taxman. If you are in business, however, your business assets could qualify for 'business property relief' when you die. If so, your **beneficiaries** will pay either no Inheritance Tax at all or only 50% of the normal rate on business assets which qualify for the relief .

This seems uncharacteristically generous of the Revenue, until you realise that only 24% of family businesses are passed on to the next generation and only 14% survive a further generation. People have a limited lifespan. The Inland Revenue is immortal and can afford to wait for its money!

The tax relief for business assets ('business property relief') will apply at 100% if you own:

o   a business as a sole trader;

o   a share in a business as a partner;

o   shares in a limited company that you cannot buy and sell on the Stock Exchange;

o   securities (loans which are secured on a company's assets) that you cannot buy and sell on the Stock Exchange, and which give you control of the company.

And the tax relief will apply at 50% if you own:

o   land, buildings, plant and machinery owned by you and used wholly or mainly in a business in which you are a partner or a company that you control;

o   shares or securities that give you control of a company listed on the Stock Exchange (you should be so lucky).

In this context, you control a company if you, or you and your spouse together, have the majority of the voting power.

1   You cannot, on your deathbed, purchase a private company to avoid Inheritance Tax. The tax relief does not apply unless you have owned it for at least two years before you die.

2   Investment companies do not qualify, so you cannot put your share portfolio into a limited company and then claim relief from Inheritance Tax. Nor can you claim relief on shares in a company through which you own buy-to-let property – but certain holiday lettings may squeak in (see p 53).

A business 'carried on otherwise than for gain' (that is, one that does not set out to make money, rather than one that sets out to make money but fails to do so!) does not qualify either.

Even if you have a business or company which qualifies for relief, the exemption may not apply to 'retained profits', that is, profits held in the business which are surplus to the business's trading requirements and, in reality, represent investment assets.

This is a sneaky one – if you in your lifetime enter into a contract to sell assets which qualify for business property relief, the Revenue will take the view that you own the sale proceeds, not the business, and are therefore fair game.

The avoidance strategy is to grant an option over the assets (which the buyer cannot exercise until after you die), rather than make a binding contract for sale. This is commonly used between business partners so that if one of them dies, the **surviving** partner(s) can exercise their option to buy out the dead partner's **beneficiaries**.

2 Agricultural property

The exemption for agricultural property ('agricultural property relief') will apply if you own:

o   agricultural land (see below: 'agriculture' is more diverse than you may think);

o   farmhouses, cottages, barns, etc 'which are of a character appropriate to the agricultural land' (see below);

o   stud farms, but not – it seems – grazing land for horses used for leisure purposes;

o   land that is used in certain limited 'habitat schemes' – that is, taken out of agricultural use and used to create a habitat for wild life. For further details on habitats, see the DEFRA paper on: www.defra.gov.uk/erdp/schemes/pre_erdp/habitat. htm.

What is agricultural land?

For your land to qualify for agricultural property relief, you must use it primarily to grow crops and/or keep livestock (including, interestingly, fish). The Valuation Office Agency – the government department responsible for valuing property for tax purposes – says that agriculture can include horticulture, fruit growing, seed growing, dairy farming, livestock breeding and keeping, land used to graze stock, meadow land, osier land, market gardens and nursery grounds, and woodlands 'where that use is ancillary to the farming of land for other agricultural purposes'. They also consider that the scope of agriculture can include the breeding and keeping of 'any creature kept for the production of food, wool, skins or fur, or for the purpose of its use in the farming of land'. So, presumably, land used for rearing angora rabbits or working farm horses would not attract Inheritance Tax.

Conversely, land whose principal purpose is not agriculture (such as a golf course, a grouse moor or a wood used for paintball war games) would not normally qualify for Inheritance Tax exemption; but farmland occasionally used for point-to-points or pop festivals probably would.

What are agricultural buildings?

In these times of low farm incomes and high property prices, the buildings on farms are often far more valuable than the land itself. Farmers may therefore be able to avoid Inheritance Tax by making sure their buildings continue to qualify for tax relief. The key concept is that the buildings should be an integral part of the farming operation. So, qualifying buildings will (to quote the Inheritance Tax Act 1984) include 'such cottages, farm buildings and farmhouses, together with the land occupied with them, as are of a character appropriate to the property'.

The 'character' of the buildings is important. A barn, battery chicken shed, pig unit or greenhouse will be exempt from Inheritance Tax because they are 'appropriate to the property', while a gazebo or a posh conservatory will almost certainly be taxable.

There are problems with farmhouses. A former farmhouse which has been sold off separately from the land will not qualify for agricultural property relief, and farmhouses, even on working farms, must be 'appropriate to the property'. A palatial farmhouse surrounded by a small 'hobby farm' is a borderline case.

Normally, farm cottages let to people who are not farm workers do not qualify for any tax relief. With cottages fetching six-figure sums, this could be bad news for your **beneficiaries**.

However, even if agricultural property relief is not available, there may be scope for business property relief (see above) instead. The Inland Revenue *may* allow business property relief (see above) on furnished holiday homes, where:

o   the lettings are short term (such as a week or a fortnight); *and*

o   the owner or their agent is (to quote the Revenue) 'substantially involved with the holidaymakers in terms of their activities on and from the premises', even if the lettings are for only part of the year.

1   You cannot, on your deathbed, purchase a farm to avoid Inheritance Tax. The tax relief does not apply unless, before you die, you have owned it:

    o   for at least two years as a working farmer; or
    o   for at least seven years while someone else has worked it.

2   As with business property relief, the usual rate of agricultural property relief is 100% (that is, no Inheritance Tax is payable at all). But if the agricultural property is let on a tenancy which began before 1 September 1995 (when there were major changes in the law relating to agricultural tenancies), the rate of relief will usually be only 50%.

3 Woodlands

But do your homework before selling your house, buying a wood and camping in it. Woodlands managed on a commercial basis qualify for business property relief (see above). Otherwise, there is a special relief for woodlands which postpones Inheritance Tax until the timber has been sold. Deathbed purchases, as with the other two headings, are not an option. You need to buy your woodland at least five years before you die.

For further information on these three exemptions, see the Inland Revenue leaflet, IHT17 *Businesses, Farms and Woodlands*, which you can download from their website www.inlandrevenue.gov.uk/leaflets/iht.htm or obtain one by post (see 'Useful contacts').

4 National heritage property

What is known as 'national heritage property' (Turner seascapes and the manuscript of *Bleak House* as well as bricks and mortar) is also exempt from Inheritance Tax, although there are not so much strings as cables attached. So if you happen to own a Grade I listed stately home, packed with art treasures of national importance, surrounded by working farmland and woods and operating as a theme park and conference centre, you may grab the entire goody bag of tax exemptions ... Otherwise, like the rest of us, you must dream on and keep rummaging around at car boot sales for your national treasure. Seriously, this example shows that the very rich can avoid Inheritance Tax more easily than the moderately prosperous.

If you think you may qualify for any of these reliefs, take professional advice. We have given you only the briefest outline of the rules.

The Inland Revenue publish a list of Extra-Statutory Concessions: items on which they are allowed to claim tax but usually choose not to. This includes 'Decorations awarded for valour or gallant conduct', which are excluded from Inheritance Tax. There is one condition: the medal, etc must be shown 'never to have been transferred for consideration in money or money's worth'. In other words, your Uncle Sid's World War II medals are exempt; the collection of militaria you have bought and swapped over the years would attract Inheritance Tax (unless, of course, the collection is of national importance or you trade in such things for a living – see above!).

More about Uncle Sid's medals on the Revenue website: go to www.inlandrevenue.gov.uk and type 'extra-statutory concessions' in the Search box.

Exempt beneficiaries

Gifts to exempt beneficiaries, both during your lifetime and on death, either in your will or as a result of the **intestacy** rules, are free of Inheritance Tax. There is no limit on the amount you give them in your lifetime or leave them when you die. But the list of exempt beneficiaries is a short one.

o **Your husband or wife**. This means that when you die, your widow or widower does not have to pay any Inheritance Tax, but see below.

1   Unmarried partners, including same-sex partners, do not qualify, and there is no such animal as a 'common law husband or wife'. However, proposed legislation may change this (see 'Equal rights?', p 15).

2   If you have your **domicile** in the UK, but your spouse is domiciled elsewhere, you can give or leave them just £55,000 free of Inheritance Tax. If you think this could apply to you, see the Inland Revenue leaflet IHT18 *Foreign Aspects*. Click on www.inlandrevenue.gov.uk/leaflets/iht.htm.

o **Charities**. All UK charities are exempt beneficiaries – but foreign charities are not. However, a gift to a UK charity which engages in charitable activities overseas will qualify. The Red Cross, for example, is an exempt beneficiary but not, it seems, Médecins sans Frontières (for further guidance on how to structure gifts to charity, see p 36).

Moreover, the following are also tax-exempt:

o Community Amateur Sports Clubs (see p 38);

o registered housing associations;

o qualifying *parliamentary* political parties;

o national museums, including the National Trust;

o universities;

o and – you've guessed it – local authorities and government departments, which would appear to include the dear old Inland Revenue!

Exempt and potentially exempt lifetime gifts

Lifetime giving (of non-exempt **assets** to non-exempt **beneficiaries**) offers considerable scope for Inheritance Tax avoidance. Some lifetime gifts are exempt even if you die the day after you hand them over, and are therefore important to deathbed tax planning. But let's start with gifts whose tax efficiency is frustrated by your premature death.

o **PETs' corner**. You must make a **potentially exempt transfer (PET)** at least seven years before your death for it to be completely free of Inheritance Tax, but even if you survive only three years from the date of the gift, there will be some taper relief.

This table shows how taper relief works.

Years between gift and death	Tax reduced by
0 – 3	No relief
3 – 4	20%
4 – 5	40%
5 – 6	60%
6 – 7	80%

If you give someone a PET and do not survive the full seven years, the recipient of the PET is the person who is liable for any Inheritance Tax on it, unless you say otherwise in your will (see 'Who pays Inheritance Tax?', p 60).

1   If you are thinking about making a PET, consider also taking out a life insurance policy which will pay the tax if you do not stay the distance (see also below on gifts from income).

2   Keep a record of the PETs you make – and particularly the dates on which you make them.

o   **Exempt lifetime gifts** – no deadline! You can give any or all of these and die next day.

o   **Gifts of not more than £3,000** in any tax year (April 6 to April 5). You can give the £3,000 all in one lump or split it into several smaller gifts totalling £3,000. You can apply all the other exceptions (so you could add it to a wedding gift) *except* the 'small gifts' exception (see below).

1   You can carry forward your unused £3,000 annual exemption from the previous tax year.

Examples

–   You made no gifts in the last tax year. In this tax year you can give away £6,000.

–   You made a gift of £2,000 in the last tax year. You can give away £4,000 this year.

2   The £3,000 annual exemption is an individual one, so couples can give away £6,000 between them in any tax year (April 6 to April 5) – or £12,000 if they have not used their allowance in the previous year.

o   **Gifts from income** – you can make as many gifts as you like out of your income after tax. To qualify, you must show that these gifts are part of your 'usual expenditure' and leave you with enough money to live on afterwards. There is no limit on amount, but there must be a pattern of 'actual or intended regular payments'.

1. Premiums on a life insurance policy written in trust can count as gifts from income. You could, for example, use such a life insurance policy to provide the fund to pay Inheritance Tax on a **PET** if you die within seven years of giving the PET. As the premiums would be gifts from income, they would be exempt from tax even if you died within the next seven years.

2. Because of the requirement for a pattern of 'actual or intended regular payments', gifts from income are all but useless for deathbed tax planning, but a single gift from income, followed by your untimely death, may qualify where it can be shown that you intended the gift to be the first of a series.

3. The Revenue advise you to 'keep some record, such as a simple account of your net income for the tax year and your expenditure, together with details of the gifts made'.

○ **Gifts for the *maintenance* of the family** – gifts for the maintenance of the following people are exempt from Inheritance Tax:

 – your spouse or ex-spouse;

 – your child or your spouse's child up to age 18 or until their full time education is complete (this includes stepchildren and adopted children);

 – other dependent relatives, for their care or maintenance. This exemption applies to any of your relatives, or your spouse's relatives, who is unable to maintain themselves because of old age or infirmity. This would include disabled grown up children and your mother or mother-in-law even if she was not elderly or infirm, unless she was living with her husband.

○ **Wedding gifts** – you can give:

 – each of your children (including adopted children and stepchildren), or the person they are marrying, up to £5,000 as a wedding gift; *and*

 – each grandchild, great-grandchild, or the person they are marrying, up to £2,500 as a wedding gift; *and*

 – anyone else, up to £1,000.

The Revenue add, 'To qualify, a wedding gift must be made on or shortly before the marriage, to one or both parties, and exemption only becomes fully effective when the marriage takes place'. So if the engagement is broken off, the money is no longer tax-exempt.

You can combine wedding gifts with your annual £3,000 exemption. For example, to a child in the year they marry, you could give £5,000 as a wedding gift and £3,000 as another gift, and these would be exempt. So a bride could receive £16,000 (£5,000 wedding gift from each parent plus £3,000 'other gift' from each parent) and the groom could receive the same from *his* parents.

o **Small gifts** – you can make as many gifts of up to £250 as you like (to different people, obviously) in any one tax year. You cannot use this with any other exemption for the same person.

You can find more information in the Inland Revenue leaflet IHT2 *Inheritance Tax on Lifetime Gifts*. Click on www.inlandrevenue.gov.uk/leaflets/iht.htm or apply by post (see 'Useful contacts').

The only Exempt Testator we can think of!

In general, anyone worth more than £263,000 who dies is a potential target for the taxman. However, if a member of the armed forces or certain associated services dies as a result of injury or disease 'received or aggravated' (the Revenue's wording) while on active service, their estate – barring PETs and certain other lifetime transfers – is exempt. This exemption does not, however, work without verification from the Ministry of Defence.

1   You may be able to save your **beneficiaries** Inheritance Tax by making lifetime gifts to them, but take care not to land yourself with a Capital Gains Tax (CGT) bill instead. A lifetime gift of a non-cash asset (such as a house which is not your main residence, or shares) is a disposal for CGT purposes. So, if the asset is what Mark describes as 'pregnant with gain', you may be liable for CGT on the notional profit after deducting your capital expenditure, cost of disposal, and making allowance for your taper relief and your annual exemption (£8,200 for individuals at the time of writing). The CGT on the disposal will be payable by you as part of your annual tax bill. Normally, of course, 'disposal' means selling and you can pay the CGT out of the proceeds of sale. In the case of a lifetime

gift on which CGT is payable, there will be no proceeds of sale, and it may be difficult for you to find the extra money to pay your CGT. So (to take an example from the Odyssey) in avoiding Scylla (the Inheritance Tax monster) you may be sucked into the whirlpool of Charybdis (CGT).

For further details of the CGT trap, see the Inland Revenue leaflet IR295 *Relief for Gifts and Similar Transactions*, available from www.inlandrevenue.gov.uk.

2   The lifetime gifts we have mentioned so far are either exempt from Inheritance Tax, or potentially exempt (**PETs**). But there is a 'lifetime rate' of Inheritance Tax – 20% – for some lifetime gifts, where the value of these gifts exceeds the **nil rate band**.

The main example is a lifetime gift to a **discretionary trust**. For instance, suppose you make a lifetime gift of £363,000 to a discretionary trust. The nil rate band is £263,000 (as of 2004/05). The taxable element of the gift is £100,000. The lifetime rate of tax is 20%, so the taxman would snatch £20,000 from *you*.

Who pays Inheritance Tax?

It is important to draw a distinction between:

o   your **estate** (the **assets** you leave after your death); and

o   non-exempt **lifetime gifts**, which have not timed out. Most commonly, such a gift will be a PET to which Inheritance tax at the 'death rate' of 40% will now apply, subject to any taper relief (see p 56) and the nil rate band.

The obligation to pay Inheritance Tax on your estate after your death lies with your **executors** (or administrators if you have no executors). They pay the tax using money they raise from your estate. Usually the tax is paid out of what is left of your estate after paying debts, costs of administration and tax-free **legacies** (if any).

But if in your lifetime you make **PET**s and die before they time out (seven years, remember), the recipients of the PETs are liable for paying the tax unless the **nil rate**

band comes to their rescue (see below) or your will states otherwise.

There is a trap here for your executors (or administrators if you do not appoint executors). If the recipient of a PET which attracts Inheritance Tax does not pay their tax bill within 12 months of your death, your executors become liable.

The nil rate band applies to gifts in chronological order – the order in which you make them.

Example: you make a PET (let's call it PET 1) of £266,000 two years *before* you die, and another PET (PET 2) of £28,000 one year before you die. You leave an estate of £10,000 *when* you die; this comprises non-exempt assets which you leave in your will to non-exempt beneficiaries.

Neither PET 1 nor PET 2 will be exempt from tax because you have died too soon. And neither qualifies for taper relief for the same reason. The recipient of PET 1 will not pay any Inheritance Tax because their PET benefits from your nil rate band of £263,000 plus your annual £3,000 exempt lifetime gift allowance. The recipient of PET 2 will benefit from your annual £3,000 exempt lifetime gift allowance, but be liable for tax at 40% on the £25,000 – that is, £10,000.

Because the nil rate band has been applied to your lifetime gifts in chronological order, there is none left for your estate on your death. Even though you have died with assets of only £10,000, there will be Inheritance Tax of £4,000 to pay on that £10,000.

The position of your beneficiaries in this example will be even worse if your will states that all tax *arising from* your death is to be paid from your estate. This would have the effect that the recipient of PET 2 will not pay tax, but there will be nothing left in your estate for your beneficiaries, because it will all have been used up to pay the tax on PET 2.

The moral is: generosity in your lifetime may, if you don't live on for seven years, penalise the people you intend to benefit in your will.

And, if you are giving a PET to someone, either:

o   make sure that the nil rate band will be sufficient to ensure there is no tax payable if you do not stay the distance; *or*

o   warn the recipient of the PET that they might get a tax bill (and consider imposing a binding obligation on them to pay that tax); *or*

o   write your will so that any tax on PETs is payable from your estate; *and/or*

o   take out life insurance (see p 83 on gifts from income).

The sample wills in this book require your executors 'to pay any taxes arising' from your death. This will include the tax on PETs which the recipients would otherwise have to pay. If you want to make a different arrangement you will have to amend the draft wills accordingly.

9

Inheritance Tax 2 – common Inheritance Tax avoidance strategies

People often think that tax planning is a magic art involving smoke and mirrors, offshore tax havens and elaborate trusts which cost a fortune to set up. In fact, the more complicated your scheme, the likelier the Revenue are to treat it as a challenge – and they have powers to unravel intricate arrangements if they believe you have made them for the sole purpose of dodging tax.

Until relatively recently, the courts would apply a strict interpretation of tax law which favoured the taxpayer. In the 1929 case of *Ayrshire Pullman Motor Services v The Commissioners of the Inland Revenue*, Lord Clyde famously remarked:

> No man in this country is under the smallest obligation, moral or other, so to arrange ... his business or his property as to enable the Inland Revenue to put the largest possible shovel into his stores.

Then, in 1981, what is known as the 'Ramsay principle' emerged from a case of the same name. The court ruled that the Inland Revenue can disregard steps taken by taxpayers which have no purpose other than avoiding paying tax. Typically this is in the context of an elaborate and pre-ordained series of transactions. The problem that taxpayers now face is that no one really knows the scope of the Ramsay principle, or the circumstances in which the Inland Revenue can use it to frustrate tax planning strategies. Legal costs being what they are, being a test case is not an attractive option!

There are slick sales teams around who offer expensive ready-made tax planning products which either sex up simple tax planning strategies to make them look like rocket science, or purvey complex and costly schemes which look (and, regrettably, usually are) too good to be true.

From 2004 the promoters of such schemes must share their secrets with the Revenue. This will allow the taxman to block the loopholes and change lawful tax avoidance into criminal tax evasion. Remember, it was tax evasion that nailed the gangster Al Capone. Do not purchase a tax-saving scheme unless the salesman can show you that it has Revenue approval.

Here is a whistle-stop tour of tax planning strategies and bloopers. We start with the strategies.

Strategy 1: Own some exempt assets

To use this strategy you need to own an exempt asset such as a business, a farm or a wood. Remember that you have to own it for a while before business property relief or agricultural property relief applies. If you want to make your home tax-exempt, consider buying a farmhouse – but of course there must be a working farm with it and the farmhouse has to be appropriate to its role (see p 5).

Strategy 2: Give away assets to exempt beneficiaries

See pp 55–56 for a list of candidates. There is no Inheritance Tax on gifts to exempt beneficiaries, whether you make them in your lifetime or on death. And if you and Him or Her Indoors have been living together for years, consider marrying them.

Strategy 3: Make exempt lifetime gifts

See the list on pp 56–57. Do bear in mind that life insurance premiums and pension contributions which carry death in service benefit will usually count as gifts from income. *Fully exempt* gifts are important for deathbed tax planning – because (unlike **PETs**) they will still be exempt even if you die very shortly after making the gifts.

Strategy 4: Make potentially exempt lifetime gifts (PETs) and survive seven years

Remember to consider who will pay the **Inheritance Tax** if you don't stay the distance. Think also about taking out life insurance to pay any tax that might otherwise cause problems either for the recipients of the **PETs** or for the **beneficiaries** of your **estate**. Even if you live only three years after giving your PET, the taper relief is worth having, and it gets better the longer you struggle on.

Strategy 5: Make non-exempt lifetime gifts which do not exceed the nil rate band

A lifetime gift to a **discretionary trust** (and also to a limited company) is not a PET, but it will fall out of your estate anyway if you live for seven years after making the gift. If the gift is more than your nil rate band (or you have already used up your nil rate band on previous non-exempt **lifetime gifts**), you will pay Inheritance Tax at the lifetime rate of 20% on the value of the gift above the nil rate band. If you then die within the seven years, additional tax on the gift will become payable (that is, the difference between the lifetime rate of 20% and the death rate of 40%).

Remember that Capital Gains Tax (CGT) may be payable on lifetime gifts of assets which are 'pregnant with gain'; but where the gift is made to a discretionary trust, the tax on the gain may be 'held over' – in which case it is not payable until the trustees dispose of the asset. Note, however, that you cannot claim hold over relief if you, as the person setting up the trust, can benefit from it. All the same, a discretionary trust can be a useful ploy, for example, for a holiday home or buy-to-let property for which 'private residence relief' does not apply. For further information about CGT and private residence relief, see the Inland Revenue's helpsheet IR283; also, for

CGT relief for gifts see IR295. Both are available from www.inlandrevenue.gov.uk. Note that to 'hold over' the gain, you have to 'elect' to do so, and notify the Inland Revenue. The form you need for the 'election' is on the back of Helpsheet IR295.

Strategy 6: Equalise assets with your spouse

You and your spouse each have a nil rate band, worth £263,000 in the 2004/05 tax year. So, if you use both nil rate bands to the full, you can give £526,000 free of Inheritance Tax to non-exempt beneficiaries, such as your children.

Obviously, you and your spouse will not be able to use both nil rate bands to the full unless each of you has assets worth a minimum of £263,000. There is no Capital Gains Tax on lifetime gifts between husband and wife, and the Revenue do not treat gifts between spouses as **GROBs**.

Unmarried partners, including same-sex partners, should also consider equalising assets for the same reason, although they need to take care that any gift between them is not a 'taxable disposal' for Capital Gains Tax purposes.

There will be circumstances in which you will not want to equalise assets completely. Suppose one of you is much older, or is in poor health. You will not want to transfer assets to them if they die before you and those assets are then caught in the taxman's net.

Take care with co-owned assets. Remember, the whole point of equalising assets is so that both you and your spouse can give the maximum amount on death to non-exempt beneficiaries, typically your children. You may defeat the object of the exercise if, when you die, your share of co-owned assets passes automatically to the surviving co-owner instead of the non-exempt beneficiaries.

Make sure, therefore, that you 'disapply the rule of survivorship' by severing the joint tenancy: we show you how to do it on p 140.

A simple but tax-efficient will gives legacies to non-exempt beneficiaries up to the value of the nil rate band (or what is left of it after taking into account lifetime gifts that have not timed out) and the residue to an exempt beneficiary – typically your spouse or a charity.

Strategy 7: Maximise your use of the nil rate band by way of gifts to non-exempt beneficiaries

The Chancellor of the Exchequer usually increases the nil rate band annually in line with the retail prices index, which in recent years has fallen far short of house price inflation, so that more and more people each year are threatened with Inheritance Tax. They are 'house rich and money poor' or, as one recent article described them, 'poor affluents'. Instead of giving fixed-sum legacies (for example, '£263,000 free of taxes to my son Marmaduke'), consider therefore giving what is known in the trade as a 'nil rate band legacy'. This is a gift to non-exempt beneficiaries of the maximum amount available within the nil rate band in force when you die, taking into account lifetime gifts that have not timed out (look at the wording in Will 8, p 179).

Strategy 8: Nil rate band discretionary trust

Suppose that you are married and have children. You would like to make a will giving your children a nil rate band legacy (see above). But if you do this, there will not be enough money for your widow or widower to live on.

The answer may be to set up what is known in the trade as a 'nil rate band **discretionary trust**' of which your widow or widower will be a potential beneficiary, as well as the children. This arrangement lets you make maximum use of your nil rate band and at the same time provides a fund for your widow or widower to live on. After they die, your children can share what is left. For an example of a nil rate band discretionary trust, see Will 9, p 182.

Strategy 9: Combine a nil rate band discretionary trust with a debt charge scheme

Phew! However, you already know about the nil rate band. In Strategy 8 we introduced the use of a discretionary trust. The only new element here is the debt charge scheme.

Here the scenario is similar to the one in Strategy 8, except that in this case the main asset is the family home. It is a truth universally acknowledged that messing around with the family home for tax planning purposes is usually undesirable and at best should be a last resort.

It is undesirable because:

o   your widow or widower, or your surviving partner, may well be vulnerable if they do not own their home outright;

o   **Capital Gains Tax (CGT)** may become payable on any profit from the sale of the home if whoever owns it (for example, your children) lives elsewhere and therefore cannot claim 'private residence relief'. For further information on private residence relief, see the Inland Revenue helpsheet IR283: go to www.inlandrevenue.gov.uk and search under IR283.

o   Beware of **GROBs**! If you make a **lifetime gift** of the family home, or a share of it, and then continue to live there without paying a market rent, the gift is likely to be ineffective as a tax saving ploy – unless, that is, the gift is to an exempt beneficiary – your husband or wife.

A nil rate band legacy (see above) consisting of the family home or a share in it poses two potential tax problems. First, there is the CGT problem: private residence relief may not be available when the home is sold if the owner lives elsewhere (see above).

Secondly, if your widow, widower or surviving partner continues to live there as a beneficiary of a **discretionary trust**, the Inland Revenue can take the view that in reality they are living there as of right, not at the trustees' discretion. In this situation, when your widow, widower or surviving partner dies, the Inland Revenue can count the value of the home as part of their estate. They have what is known in the trade as an 'interest in possession' on which Inheritance Tax is payable, just as if they own the asset outright.

The way around this problem is asset substitution. The problem is *caused* by having the family home, or a share in it, as an asset of the nil rate band discretionary trust (see above). The problem is *solved* by having a loan – which may be secured on the family home, like a mortgage – as the trust's main asset instead of the home itself, of which your widow, widower or surviving partner becomes the sole owner.

Here is how it works:

o   The trustees *lend* to your widow, widower or surviving partner an amount equal to the nil rate band legacy. Of course, they never see any actual money!

o   The loan, which is usually interest free, is repaid when your widow, widower or surviving partner dies.

No money actually changes hands – the transaction is all on paper; but the result for the taxman is:

o   no CGT: your widow, widower or surviving partner will own the home outright, and providing it continues to be their main residence, there will be no CGT to pay on sale;

o   no Inheritance Tax: the Inland Revenue will not be able to claim that because your widow, widower or surviving partner is living in the family home there is an 'interest in possession' in the assets of the discretionary trust.

There is a degree of artificiality here (see our comments on Ramsay, above), and the scheme has not been tested in court, but the Revenue appears so far to accept it as valid.

Strategy 10: Post-death variation

Your 'last will and testament' need not be the Last Word! After you die, your **executors** and your adult **beneficiaries** are allowed, in effect, to rewrite your will using a 'deed of variation'. They can do this so far as the rewriting does not reduce the share of any beneficiary who is under 18 or unable or unwilling to give informed consent to the changes.

This facility can be used for a number of purposes, such as:

o   to improve the tax efficiency of your will;

o   to right wrongs – if you have left someone short, the other beneficiaries can see them right;

o   to pre-empt a claim under the Inheritance (etc) Act (see p 18);

o   to skip a generation (see below).

Typical situations where a deed of variation could improve tax efficiency are where:

o   your will has left everything to your widow or widower. The deed of variation introduces a **legacy** to non-exempt beneficiaries such as your children, thus making use of your nil rate band;

o   your will has left too much money to non-exempt beneficiaries, such as your children. The deed of variation restricts their share to a **nil rate band** legacy and gives the **residue** to your widow or widower (both are exempt beneficiaries, with the result that there is no **Inheritance Tax** on the residue).

For capital tax (Inheritance Tax and CGT) purposes, the changes will take effect as if you had made them in your will – as long as:

o   the variation is made in writing; *and*

o   all the beneficiaries who will lose out sign the variation; *and*

o   the variation is made within two years of your death; *and*

o   the variation contains a statement that it takes effect for capital tax purposes; *and* o   the changes relate only to assets in your **estate** (so a beneficiary cannot swap something in your estate for an asset they already own, or use their own money to buy another beneficiary's share in your estate); *and*

o   if, as a result of the variation, there is more Inheritance Tax to pay, the executors must also sign; *and*

o   the variation must contain a statement that it is exempt from Stamp Duty. There is a standard form of words for this.

Note that a deed of variation is not restricted to wills. It can be used to:

o   vary an **intestacy**;

o   sever a joint tenancy (see the Inland Revenue's comments on this in Tax Bulletin 19, available at www.inlandrevenue.gov.uk).

Your beneficiaries can make more than one variation, as long as any later variation does not affect the same assets – they can't tinker more than once with the same asset.

For more information about deeds of variation, see the Inland Revenue's clear and helpful leaflet IHT8, available on their website. If your executors/ beneficiaries are minded to vary your will, they should take professional advice. (For a draft deed of variation, see p 186.)

Strategy 11: Generation skipping

Not a competitive sport, but a common **Inheritance Tax** avoidance ploy. The concept is straightforward. Your family will pay less Inheritance Tax if you skip a generation and leave your assets, for example, to grandchildren rather than children. This might be particularly relevant if:

o   your children are already well provided for;

o   your children are in poor health;

o   your children are useless with money (although strictly speaking you may not save Inheritance Tax by cutting them out of your will, you may at least be able to preserve your assets for the grandchildren in the hope that they will be thriftier).

If your grandchildren are under 18, consider setting up a **trust** for them either in your lifetime or in your will.

Strategy 12: Living off capital

To do this effectively you need a crystal ball.

You can get along on less than you think you need, if you are prepared to use your capital to supplement your income. Of course, as you eat into your savings your remaining capital will generate less income. But if you are already old (say, over 80) this may be a reasonable strategy because you are unlikely to outlive your money. You can then make lifetime gifts of surplus assets (see pp 55–60).

Strategy 13: More tax planning options for the family home

o   Downsizing: if you are an empty-nester and your home and/or garden is now too large for your needs, consider moving to a smaller home and making a lifetime gift to your children of the surplus sale proceeds. There will be no CGT on the sale because of private residence relief. Then check what exempt lifetime gifts you can make (at the very least, your annual exempt amount should be available). You can then give away the rest as a **PET** – tax free if you live seven years.

o   Sharing: if you have a grown up child who still lives with you in the family home (with or without a spouse or partner) and the arrangement is likely to be permanent, consider making them a lifetime gift of a share in the home. No CGT will be payable on the gift, and if the home is sold, both you and your child will also benefit from private residence relief. Again, check what exempt lifetime gifts you have available to you. The rest of the gift will be a **PET** rather than a **GROB** – as long as each sharing owner lives there and pays their share of expenses. It is especially important that you as the giver continue to pay your share.

o   Conversion: if there is scope for converting the family home into two or more units, you might be able to live in one unit and give the others away to your grown up child. Think about CGT issues which will arise when they sell. If your child lives in the other unit, they will benefit from private residence relief when they sell up.

Note that you will need planning permission for any conversion or change of use. As a result of getting permission, you may well increase the value of the property. If your child expects to rent out their unit, you should keep the whole property in *your* name until planning permission has been granted, because in your hands any increase in value as a result of the permission may well be protected from CGT by your private residence relief.

Strategy 14: Deathbed planning

This is all about making the best use of exempt **lifetime gifts** at the last moment.

Bear in mind that a useful feature of CGT (to your beneficiaries, that is, rather than to the taxman) is that when you die there will be no CGT to pay on the value of your capital assets at death – even those on which you would have paid CGT if you had sold them at a profit in your lifetime. So, if you own assets which are 'pregnant with gain', hold onto them until you die to avoid CGT on sale. More cunningly, if your spouse owns assets which are 'pregnant with gain', arrange for those assets to be transferred to you while you are still alive, so that your death will 'wash the gain'.

Keep tax saving in proportion

And finally, even if you are rich enough to worry about **Inheritance Tax**, do try to keep a sense of proportion about your tax liability. In theory, it is often possible to avoid or reduce Inheritance Tax by reducing the value of your estate. In practice, this is often difficult to do because you may only be able to avoid the tax by giving away your home in your lifetime or giving away the savings which are important to your income. Don't deprive yourself, or someone you love, for a small tax saving.

10

Common Inheritance Tax bloopers

In matters of **Inheritance Tax** planning, just as there is scope for strategy, there is also potential for getting things expensively *wrong*. If you decide to launch into Inheritance Tax planning and you are not sure what you are doing (like DIY plumbing/electrics really), do consider taking professional advice from someone, such as a solicitor or a chartered accountant, whose advice is backed by indemnity insurance. Even if the professional just 'blesses' what you have thought up for yourself and want to do, the professional will carry the risk of any bloopers – that's what you are paying them for!

Beware of free advice. TANSTAAFL – there ain't no such thing as a free lunch. 'Free' advice is usually sales talk, and is usually worth what you pay for it.

Here is a list of common traps for the unwary but, unlike the potential for human error, it is not exhaustive.

Lifetime gifts that bite back

Blooper 1: Capital Gains Tax (CGT) on lifetime gifts

Remember that a **lifetime gift** of a non-cash **asset** (such as a house which is not your main residence, or shares) is a disposal for CGT purposes. So, if the asset is 'pregnant with gain', you may be liable for CGT on the notional profit, after deducting allowable expenditure and costs, and using whatever reliefs and exemptions might be available to you.

Normally, of course, 'disposal' means selling and you can pay the CGT out of the proceeds of sale. In the case of a lifetime gift on which CGT is payable, there will be no proceeds of sale, and it may be difficult for you to find the extra money to pay the CGT.

This is especially costly if you then die shortly after making the gift, with the result that your **executors** pay CGT and Inheritance Tax on the same asset.

How to convert an exempt asset (such as a business or farm) into a monstrous tax bill in two easy steps:

1   Sell the exempt asset during your lifetime, and pay CGT on the profit (although the rate of tax may in fact be modest if, for example, the special low rate of taper relief for business assets applies).

2   Die shortly afterwards, and land your executors with the Inheritance Tax bill on the proceeds of sale.

It's easy when you know how!

Blooper 2: GROBs

A **GROB**, you will recall, is a Gift with Reservation of Benefit. This is a gift you make in your lifetime from which you keep back some benefit. Common examples are:

o   a lifetime gift – on paper only – of your home. If you still live in it afterwards and do not pay a market rent, you have given a GROB;

o   lifetime gifts of furniture, jewellery, pictures or other works of art that stay in your home instead of going to their supposed recipients;

o   a lifetime gift of a holiday home which you continue to use rent free instead of handing over the only set of keys to the supposed recipient.

GROBs do not work for **Inheritance Tax** purposes – the value of the asset is simply added back into your **estate** when you die (unless, that is, the gift is to an exempt **beneficiary** – your husband or wife). You can read more about the Inland Revenue's interpretation of GROBs in Tax Bulletin 9 available at www.inlandrevenue.gov.uk/

bulletins/tb9.htm. There have been elaborate schemes available by which you can make a lifetime gift and enjoy the benefit without – technically at least – giving a GROB. In the 2004 Budget, the Chancellor announced plans to levy income tax on any benefit you retain.

Blooper 3: Lifetime gift and loan back

Suppose you have the clever idea of giving your adult child (who will also inherit under your will) £100,000 – and immediately borrowing it back. There are two reasons why this apparently attractive ploy will not work:

o   Unless the loan is on commercial terms and you pay a market rate of interest, the gift will be a GROB (see above).

o   In any case, the Inland Revenue will, for Inheritance Tax purposes, disregard the loan when you die if your child is one of your beneficiaries. Your executors will, of course, still have to repay the loan to your child. But in calculating the value of your estate on which Inheritance Tax is payable, your executors will not be able to deduct the £100,000 as a liability of your estate.

A second trap arises where you make a **PET (Potentially Exempt Transfer)** of a property to your adult child, buy it back from them at market value, but never actually hand over any money – so a loan equal to the purchase price would seem to be a debt of your estate. The Inland Revenue, however – spoilsports that they are – will disregard this 'artificial debt', which will not be deductible in calculating your taxable estate.

There is a third trap where you make a PET of a property to your adult child and buy it back from them at market value. At the time, you do not actually pay anything. Later you repay the debt. The Revenue will treat the repayment itself as a PET – so it will not be tax-deductible unless you survive seven years.

Blooper 4: Not working out who will pay Inheritance Tax on PETs

If you make a **PET** in your lifetime and die before it times out (seven years, remember), the recipient of the PET is liable for paying the tax unless the **nil rate band** comes to their rescue or your will states otherwise (see p 60 on 'Who pays Inheritance Tax?'). But if the recipient of the PET does not pay their tax bill within 12 months of your death, your executors become liable. It will save a lot of grief if you make provision for the tax by way of a life insurance policy, if this is available on terms you can afford (see pp 57–58 on 'Gifts from income'). Otherwise, you need to make it clear when you give the PET who will pay the tax in the event of your untimely death, and make sure that the terms of your will are consistent with this.

Squandering your nil rate band

Blooper 5: 'Bunching' of assets

You and your spouse each have a nil rate band, worth £263,000 in the 2004/05 tax year. So, if you use both nil rate bands to the full, you can give £526,000 free of Inheritance Tax to non-exempt beneficiaries, such as your children.

Obviously, you and your spouse will not be able to use both nil rate bands to the full unless each of you has assets worth a minimum of £263,000 (see Strategy 6 above).

'Bunching' occurs where one spouse (or partner) has all the wealth. If the 'poor' spouse or partner dies first, the opportunity to use that person's nil rate band to make a tax-free gift to non-exempt beneficiaries is lost forever.

Bunching of jointly owned assets

Where the rule of survivorship applies, and you co-own assets as a joint tenant, the deceased co-owner's share passes automatically to the other co-owner(s), regardless of anything you say in your will. If you intend, in your will, to give your share of a co-owned asset in a nil rate band **legacy** to a non-exempt beneficiary (such as your child), instead of to the other co-owner (such as your husband or wife), the gift will be ineffective if the rule of survivorship applies. On your death, the value of the entire asset will be 'bunched' in the hands of the co-owner(s) and your nil rate band will be wasted.

The fix here is to make sure that the rule of survivorship does not apply, by 'severing the joint tenancy'. We show you how on pp 139–40. Even after your death, it is still not necessarily too late to sever the joint tenancy (see Strategies 6 and 10).

Squandering your exempt assets

An **exempt asset**, you will recall, is one which qualifies for exemption from **Inheritance Tax**. Examples can be business assets and farmland.

The great advantage of an exempt asset is that no tax will be payable when you hand it on, no matter how much it is worth. So, if you have a qualifying business worth, say, £12 million, there is no messing about with nil rate bands – the whole lot is out of the taxman's reach.

Blooper 6: Converting an exempt asset into a non-exempt one

It sounds difficult, but you can do it if you try. The prize blooper is to sell the asset, convert it into cash and watch the vultures circle.

Another example might be if you own a farm with a farmhouse of what the Revenue call 'an appropriate character' and convert the house into Southfork or a Venetian palazzo.

1   If you in your lifetime enter into a contract to sell assets which qualify for business property relief or agricultural property relief, the Revenue will take the view that you own the sale proceeds, not the business, and are therefore fair game. See p 51 to find out how to avoid this, by using an option instead of a contract.

2   Beware of an exempt asset (your farm or business) mutating into a non-exempt one in the form of large sums of money in accrued profits. Plough the profits back into the business, or take them out. Don't leave them in the business account for the taxman.

3   The best blooper here is to give a legacy in your will of what you mistakenly believe is an exempt asset, and say in your will that the legacy is free of tax. You get it wrong – the gift is subject to tax after all, and as a result of your making the gift free of tax, the beneficiaries of the residue of your estate, not the recipient of the legacy, pay the tax! Family vendettas have ignited over less!

Blooper 7: Giving an exempt asset to an exempt beneficiary

There may be perfectly good personal or commercial reasons for you to give your business to your spouse, but you would make better use of your business property relief if you gave it to a non-exempt beneficiary, such as your adult child, instead.

Treasure your exempt assets, because they do not lug a burden of tax with them. As well as the exemption from Inheritance Tax, business and agricultural assets enjoy favourable CGT treatment too. If you plan to make a gift to a charity (another exempt beneficiary), and your estate is a mixture of exempt and non-exempt assets, you will increase the tax efficiency of your will if you give a non-exempt asset to the charity and save the exempt ones for your children. Then neither will be a target for the taxman.

Blooper 8: Making a nil rate band gift which (unknown to you) includes exempt assets

Let us say that you have made a will with a nil rate band legacy to your children. You also own business assets which you intend to give, as part of the residue of your estate, to your partner. You express the nil rate band legacy to give to your children the maximum they can have free of tax. The legacy will include the business assets, because those assets, being exempt, will also be free of tax. This deprives your partner of the business assets.

The solution is to express the nil rate band legacy as the maximum amount of *cash* you can give to your children free of tax.

Neglecting your exempt beneficiaries

Your spouse is an exempt beneficiary – you can give them as much as you like both in your lifetime and in your will, without paying tax. The same goes for charities.

Blooper 9: Giving everything to non-exempt beneficiaries

Suppose you are married, with adult children. You are wealthy. As your husband or wife is also wealthy in their own right, you write a will leaving everything to the children. They will have to pay Inheritance Tax on the value of your taxable estate above the nil rate band.

The tax-efficient strategy would be to give the children a nil rate band legacy and leave the residue of your estate to your spouse. Your spouse makes a **mirror will**. Result: no tax is payable on the 'first death' – although of course there will be tax on the 'second death' on the value of the estate above the nil rate band – unless the widow or widower has taken further tax avoidance precautions (see Chapter 9 for suggestions).

If there is a significant age difference between you and your spouse, then a gift of assets to whichever of you is younger would also make sense.

We have already said (see Strategy 9) that messing around with the family home for tax planning purposes is usually undesirable and at best should be a last resort.

Messing about with the family home

Blooper 10: Losing private residence relief on the family home

You do not pay CGT when you sell or give away your home, thanks to 'private residence relief'. For more information on this, see Strategy 9. However, CGT may become payable on any profit from the sale of the home if whoever owns it (for example, your children) lives elsewhere and therefore cannot claim this relief. Do not, therefore, give your home to someone who is not going to live there. While such a ploy may save **Inheritance Tax** (as long as it is not a **GROB** – see Blooper 2), it could land the recipients with a CGT bill instead.

Blooper 11: Creating an 'interest in possession' in the family home

In Strategy 8, we explained how to use a nil rate band discretionary trust to provide financially for your widow or widower, and at the same time make maximum use of your nil rate band. In Strategy 9 we showed how to apply this arrangement to the family home or a share in it. The potential blooper occurs where the family home, or a share in it, is an asset of the discretionary trust in which the widow or widower acquires an 'interest in possession'. The result is that the value of the family home is added to the widow or widower's estate for Inheritance Tax purposes when they die. The solution, as we explained in Strategy 9, is to use a debt charge scheme.

Stragglers

Here are a few bloopers which don't fit into the other categories and don't rate a category of their own.

Blooper 12: Life insurance proceeds that attract Inheritance Tax

We have explained that the premiums you pay on your life insurance will count as 'gifts out of income' and are therefore exempt from **Inheritance Tax**. You can also make sure that the proceeds of the policy do not form part of your **estate** when you die by writing the policy in trust. In other words, the policy names the person who will receive the proceeds when you die. The proceeds will therefore be free of Inheritance Tax.

The blooper is not to write the policy in trust – that is, forget to name the person who is to receive the proceeds. When you die, therefore, the proceeds will be part of your taxable estate.

1   Many people have mortgage protection policies, which will repay the mortgage if they die during the term of the mortgage. It may be preferable to write the policy in trust for, say, your co-owner.

2   If you are in work and have a pension scheme which provides death in service benefit, remember to let the **trustees** of the scheme know who is to receive the lump sum if you die before drawing your pension (for more about this, see p 15).

Blooper 13: Gifts to children that cost you money

Lifetime gifts from parents to their children under 18 do not come with any income tax benefit. The child's income from the gift income is treated as the parent's income until the child turns 18. There is an exemption, however, for assets which produce income of no more than £100 a year. But you cannot make use of the child's annual individual income tax allowance, which in the current tax year (2004/05) is £4,745.

The position is different for grandchildren. If you make a lifetime gift to your grandchildren, the income from the gift is treated as their income and they have the full individual annual income tax allowance (see above) even while they are under 18.

If you still want to make a gift to your own children before they turn 18, consider setting up an accumulation and maintenance trust (see p 99).

Getting tax saving out of proportion

You may well find that there is a conflict between providing responsibly for yourself, your family and your dependants on the one hand and efficient tax planning on the other. It may be impossible to have it both ways. In these circumstances, it may well be better for your beneficiaries to pay at least some tax at some future date than to make financial arrangements which create more problems than they solve.

Blooper 14: Saving tax but losing money

(Throwing the baby out with the bath water?) There is no point in making tax saving arrangements which just create other problems. Examples are:

o   losing control of assets which you need to live on;

o   making gifts to feckless or bankrupt beneficiaries (for more on this subject, see p 35).

Blooper 15: Beggaring yourself or, worse, your widow or widower, to save tax

No comment!

Life insurance

How to be worth more dead than alive

Will your net **estate** after you die be enough:

o   to pay your debts, such as your mortgage?

o   to take care of your children until they can take care of themselves?

o   to support your partner or other dependants, such as your young children?

Of course, there never seems to be enough money to go round, but at least with life insurance you can make sure you are worth more dead than alive. Bear in mind that there are three types of life insurance. These are, in order of cost:

o   **Term insurance**: this insures your life for a fixed period of time, at the end of which you do not receive any return on your money. The insurers do not pay out unless you die within the fixed period. The policy has no more investment value than a betting ticket. You bet you'll die by a certain date, in which case they pay out. They bet you'll struggle on past the deadline (sorry) and thus lose your premiums (and, of course, your bet!).

o   **Whole-life insurance**: this pays out when you die (whenever that is).

o   **Endowment insurance**: this pays out when you die, or at the end of a fixed period of time, whichever is earlier. Endowment policies have historically been linked with mortgages. During the period of the mortgage, you just pay interest on your loan, and you do not repay the capital. At the same time as taking on the mortgage, you take out an endowment insurance policy which will pay out when the mortgage ends or when you die, whichever is sooner. The theory is that the proceeds of the policy will be enough to repay the loan. Recently, however, many home buyers with endowment mortgages have been left with shortfalls when the policy proceeds were not sufficient to repay their loans.

Bear in mind that whole-life and endowment insurances are, in effect, combined insurance and investment products. The problem is one of *transparency*: the return which you get on the policy may not reflect the underlying performance of the assets that the insurer holds on your behalf. In bad times, this may benefit you, because the insurers do not deduct investment losses from the value of your policy. But in good times it means they may not be passing on the profits they make on *your* money.

Life insurance can be used – and misused – in **Inheritance Tax** planning (see Chapters 9 and 10), as can:

o   death in service benefit policies (see p 15) if you are in work; and

o   mortgage protection policies (in practice, mortgage lenders urge you take one out when you take on your mortgage).

The financial services industry also peddles sophisticated trust schemes which claim to enable older people to give away capital and have enough income to live on at the same time. But see our comments on smoke and mirrors on p 63 before parting with any money.

Getting the right advice

Go to an independent financial adviser, and shop around. There are websites which will help you to do this. A certain amount of 'web wisdom' is required here. If you key in 'independent financial adviser' on the web you will be spoilt for choice. Instead, start with the Financial Services Authority (FSA): www.fsa.gov.uk. The

FSA describes itself as 'the independent watchdog set up by the Government to regulate financial services and protect your rights'. It offers a useful booklet, *You and Your Money*, and an online search facility to enable you to check whether a financial adviser is a member of the FSA. There is also a helpline: 0845 606 1234.

Key in SOFA – the Society of Financial Advisers on www.sofa.org or www.unbiased.co.uk – for financial advisers near you, whom you will of course check out on the FSA site to make sure they are FSA members!

Note that there are two main types of financial adviser (Rosy says, 'Those who suck your toes and those who suck your blood'!):

o tied agents, who offer the products of only one financial institution; and

o independent advisers, who can recommend products from the whole range available.

Superficially, an independent adviser sounds a better proposition than a tied agent; however, tied agents are more likely to be employed on a straight salary basis, whereas independent advisers are usually on commission, which, they will assure you, never influences their recommendations. In fact, most people selling insurance, independent or otherwise, are on commission. Could it be that the policy that the salesman is pushing is by any chance the one which gets him the juiciest cut?

12

Trusts

Why are we putting a chapter on trusts in a book about wills? There are two reasons:

o   Many wills involve some form of trust, even if the word 'trust' does not appear in the will. Examples are:

   –   an age-**contingent** gift to a child (for example, 'my daughter Natalie on attaining the age of 18 years') creates what is known as an *accumulation and maintenance trust* (see below);

   –   a gift to someone who does not have the mental capacity to handle money should always be made in trust. In draft Will 7 we provide a form of **discretionary trust** for a child with a mental disability.

o   Trusts have their uses in tax planning. The popular myth is that a trust is a sort of magical fortress, often on an offshore island, where no one ever pays any tax and wizards' spells and lawyers' runes protect your money from the taxman.

   You wish! Except for the mega-rich, who can afford to live by different rules from the rest of us, trusts aren't like that at all. But they do have their place in tax planning, and in Chapter 9 on 'strategies' you can see how, for example, we use a discretionary trust as a tax-saving ploy.

A trust is a legal arrangement which imposes a duty on someone – the **trustee** – to own and manage assets for the benefit of someone else – the **beneficiary** – usually on a long term basis. An **executor** is a form of trustee with specific, short term responsibilities relating to the administration of the dead person's estate. Where a trust is set up which can provide for several beneficiaries in turn, the arrangement is usually known as a *settlement*, and the person who sets this arrangement up is known as the *settlor*. The **assets** in a settlement are often described as *settled property* or as a *trust fund*, which is the term we prefer.

When someone receives the Queen's Commission as an officer in the armed forces, or is installed as Chancellor of a university, they are described as 'trusty and well beloved'. This sums up the ethos of being a trustee – someone who has special responsibilities which they must discharge in utmost good faith (even when no one is looking!) and with 'reasonable skill and care'. For a non-professional trustee, 'reasonable skill and care' means the standard of skill and care they would use in their own affairs – which may include taking expert advice. The standard of skill and care expected of a professional trustee is higher – that of a competent member of their profession.

Many relationships involve 'good faith'. However, a trustee's relationship with their beneficiary is one of 'utmost good faith – *uberrimae fidei*'. This demands the highest standards of integrity. A trustee must put the beneficiary's interests first at all times. They must be not only clean, but squeaky clean.

As well as private trusts (like the ones people set up for their families in their wills), financial institutions, such as pension funds, use trusts to hold funds for their clients, and charities are often set up in the form of a trust. Many of the basic principles of trust law apply to all forms of trust, whatever their size.

Duties

Trustees of private trusts have the following duties:

o To invest the trust fund responsibly. In fact, trustees have statutory duties to choose suitable investments, not to put all the trust fund's eggs in one basket, and to keep an eye on their progress. In practice, for non-professional trustees this means taking expert advice.

o To keep accounts, and to show them to the beneficiaries on request. In practice, the trustees will need accounts anyway so that they can complete tax returns.

o To conserve trust assets, which in the case of **real estate** means maintaining and insuring them.

o To avoid personal gain at the beneficiaries' expense: sometimes called 'the duty not to profit', which sums it up nicely. This means that trustees must not put themselves in a position where their interests conflict, either actually or potentially, with those of the trust. As a result, trustees are generally forbidden to acquire assets from the trust, and non-professional trustees cannot charge for their services.

o To distribute income and/or capital in accordance with the terms of the trust, impartially and to the correct beneficiaries.

Decisions

There will normally be at least two trustees in charge of a trust fund, so with luck they can police each other. The decisions they make must be unanimous, and obviously what they decide to do will be governed both by the general law of trusts and by the particular terms of the trust they administer. Although trustees do have the right to delegate some of their functions, as a general principle they must make their own decisions – they can't pass the buck, although, of course, they can and should take advice.

Powers

Trustees of private trusts usually have the following specific powers:

o to use the trust income for the education and maintenance of a beneficiary under 18;

o to hand over the capital of the trust fund to beneficiaries, if it is in the beneficiaries' interests to do so. The trustees can hand over capital to an adult beneficiary even if the beneficiary has an age-**contingent** interest in the trust and has not yet reached that age. They can also hand money over to the parents or guardian of a beneficiary under 18.

What kind of trust?

In this chapter we describe the main forms of trust available to UK residents, their uses and the way each one is taxed.

Bare trust

As its name implies, this kind of trust offers 'the bare necessities'. It is really a nominee arrangement, by which an **asset** belonging to one person is in the name of another. In a bare **trust**, the **beneficiary** is the absolute owner and the trustees just do what they are told.

Uses

The main use of a bare trust is to give an asset to someone under 18 which they cannot hold in their own name (precisely because they *are* under 18). The advantage of a bare trust is that the income and capital gains belong to the beneficiary, and the beneficiary's income tax and Capital Gains Tax (CGT) allowances can be claimed on their behalf.

1   The main problem with a bare trust is that a **beneficiary** who is feckless with money, or too young to handle money, can get at the trust fund and waste it. The trustees are powerless to prevent this.

2   **Lifetime gifts** from parents to their children under 18 do not come with any income tax benefit. The child's income from the gift income is treated as the parent's income until the child turns 18. There is an exemption, however, for assets which produce income of no more than £100 a year. But you cannot make use of the child's annual individual income tax allowance, which in the current tax year (2004/05) is £4,745.

The tax position is different for grandchildren. If you make a lifetime gift to your grandchildren, the income from the gift is treated as their income and they have the full individual annual income tax allowance (see above) even while they are under 18.

Interest in possession trust

This is a **trust** which gives the **beneficiary** the right to income from a trust fund, usually (but not always) for life. The beneficiary does not have the right to the capital but the trustees usually have a discretion to dole out capital when required (such as for a deposit on a house).

In the film *Doctor in the House* the medical student played by Kenneth More always drank a toast to Mrs Rivington-Lomax, who had left him £500 a year for the duration of his medical training. When the story began, the lad was on approximately his 10th resit ... Although this is fiction, it's still a good illustration of an interest in possession trust which was intended to confer less than a life interest. The student did eventually pass his exams.

These days, interest in possession trusts have, to some extent, fallen out of favour because of their **Inheritance Tax** implications. If you are the beneficiary of an interest in possession trust, the value of the capital will be added to your estate for Inheritance Tax purposes when you die.

All the same, interest in possession trusts still have their uses – although not for tax planning. Here are some situations in which you might consider an interest in possession trust:

o   Suppose you have married for the second time and have children from your first marriage. In effect, you have two families, and you have conflicting financial obligations to both of them. You might want to write a will giving your second spouse the right to income, or the right to live in the family home, for life. After they die, the capital will then go to your children by both marriages. The snag with this type of arrangement is that it tends to set your widow or widower and the children of your first marriage at each other's throats. Your widow or widower will want to maintain their standard of living, but your children of your first marriage will see this as squandering their inheritance.

o Suppose you and your spouse are elderly and infirm. You own your own home. You are concerned that when one of you dies, the other will have to go into residential care. If your widow or widower has an interest in possession trust in the family home, and therefore has the right to live there for life, the authorities will not be able to force the sale of the house, or put a charge on it, to pay for care fees.

Taxation of an interest in possession trust

Income Tax

There are two possibilities. The simplest arrangement is for the beneficiary to receive the income of the trust direct. The trustees are then said to have 'mandated' the income to the beneficiary. In that case, the beneficiary declares the income on their tax return and can claim their annual allowance and any other reliefs they are entitled to. Otherwise, where the trustees receive the income, they pay income tax at the savings rate (20% in 2004/05) or basic rate (22% in 2004/05), depending on the source of income. The trustees then pass the net income to the beneficiary. If the beneficiary is a higher rate taxpayer, they may have to pay more tax on their income from the trust.

Capital Gains Tax

Most interest in possession trusts are set up in wills. If, however, you create one in your lifetime, the gift of assets to the trust may count as a disposal for CGT purposes (see the Inland Revenue helpsheet IR295, available from www.inlandrevenue.gov.uk).

If the trustees sell assets at a profit, CGT may also be payable. The trustees' annual exemption (the amount of profit they are allowed to make on the sale without paying tax) is only half that of an individual – just £4,100 in 2004/05 instead of £8,200. Trustees have their own special rate of tax, known as the RAT (rate applicable to trusts), which is 40%.

If the trustees hand over assets to the beneficiary, this gift may also count as a disposal for CGT purposes (see above).

Inheritance Tax

As we said, most interest in possession trusts are set up in wills. But if you create one in your lifetime, the gift of assets to the trust will count as a **PET** and time out for Inheritance Tax purposes in seven years. Once the asset is in the trust, it is counted in the beneficiary's estate when they die (see above).

Discretionary trust

A **discretionary trust** lets the trustees decide who gets what, and when they will get it. Under a discretionary trust, there will be a list of potential **beneficiaries** but none of them will have the right to receive anything unless the **trustees** make a decision in their favour. Where trustees decide to give income or capital, this is sometimes known (pure law-speak) as an 'appointment'.

Discretionary trusts are useful in situations where:

o   you wish to provide for a financially improvident beneficiary (see 'Bankrupt and irresponsible beneficiaries', p 35);

o   you wish to provide for a beneficiary with a mental disability (see p 32 and Will 7, p 173). This type of discretionary trust has especially favourable tax treatment;

o   you are 'house rich and money poor'. You wish to make full use of your own nil rate band (£263,000 in 2004/05) when you die, but if you do so your widow or widower may not have enough money to live on. The solution may be a **nil rate band** discretionary trust (see Strategy 7, p 67);

o   you want to make a **lifetime gift** of an **asset**, such as a second home, which is 'pregnant with gain'. The problem is that if you give the asset directly to the beneficiary, the gift will count as a disposal of the asset for CGT purposes and tax may be payable even though you have no proceeds of sale from which to pay the tax. If, however, you hand the asset to a discretionary trust, there should be 'hold-over relief' (see Strategy 5, p 65);

○ you can't make up your mind who should get what, possibly because at the time you make your will it is not clear what each person's financial circumstances will be when you die. Alternatively, you may genuinely want someone else to make a difficult decision for you. The answer is known as a 'two-year discretionary trust'. Under this arrangement, the trustees have two years from your death to get their act together – to decide who should have what. As long as the trustees do this within the two year time limit, the gifts they make take effect, for **Inheritance Tax** purposes, as if you had made them in your will.

1   To comply with the arcane technicalities of tax law, your trustees should not make their decisions within the three months immediately following your death.

2   Strictly speaking, it appears that your trustees are not allowed to make a decision about what happens to your assets until they actually have control of them. So your executors should get a move on – they need to wind up your estate before the two-year deadline.

3   It is prudent to include a default gift, which will take effect if your trustees do time out. In fact, this point applies to most discretionary trusts – you need to say what should happen to the trust fund if the trustees do not make up their minds, or if the potential beneficiaries die.

Income Tax

The RAT (see above) will nibble at the income from the trust fund at 40%, except on dividend income, which is taxed at 32.5%.

Capital Gains Tax

If you set up a discretionary trust in your lifetime, the gift of assets to the trust will count as a disposal for CGT purposes – but 'hold-over relief' may apply (see 'Track changes!', p viii).

If the trustees sell assets at a profit, or hand over assets to beneficiaries, CGT may also be payable. The position is the same as for interest in possession trusts (see above), with one exception: when the trustees of a discretionary trust hand over assets to the beneficiaries, hold-over relief (see Strategy 5, p 65) may be available. This is because Inheritance Tax may be payable on the handover (see below) and the general rule is that Inheritance Tax and CGT are not payable on the same transaction. Hold-over relief is not available where a disposal is made within three months of a 10-yearly charge (see 'Happy birthday!' below).

Moreover, hold-over relief is not available on a distribution from a discretionary trust set up by a will within two years of death (but see p 96 on the Inheritance Tax advantages of two-year discretionary trusts). Swings and roundabouts ...

Inheritance Tax

If, during your lifetime, you set up a discretionary trust, Inheritance Tax at the lifetime rate of 20% is payable on your gift of assets to the trust so far as the value of the gift is greater than your available nil rate band.

For example:

Twenty years ago you bought a holiday home for £25,000. 'Dungraftin' is now worth £313,000. You realise that if you give it to your children during your lifetime, there will be CGT to pay on the disposal, so you decide to put 'Dungraftin' into a discretionary trust during your lifetime instead. You have not previously used any of your nil rate band. The full £263,000 is therefore available. There will be Inheritance Tax to pay of £10,000 – that is, 20% (the lifetime rate of Inheritance Tax) of £50,000, which is the part of 'Dungraftin' that pokes above the nil rate band. For further details, see Strategy 5 on p 65.

Happy birthday!

Every 10 years, an official in the Capital Taxes Office (Inheritance Tax subdivision) of the Revenue remembers your discretionary trust's birthday and extorts what is known as the '10-yearly charge'. This is, broadly speaking, a charge on:

- the value of the trust on its relevant birthday (that is, 10th, 20th, 30th, and so on); *plus*
- the value (at the time they began) of any other trusts set up by the same person ('settlor') on the same day; *plus*
- the value of PETs and non-exempt lifetime gifts made by the same person in the seven years before setting up the discretionary trust.

The rate of tax is 6% of the value of the assets concerned, so far as this value is higher than the nil rate band on the trust's relevant birthday. For further information about how to calculate the 10-yearly charge, see the Inland Revenue's leaflet IHT16 *Inheritance Tax on Settled Property*, available from www.inlandrevenue.gov.uk.

You will notice that the 10-year charge applies to the value of other trusts set up by the same person on the same day – these are known as 'related settlements'. Where a discretionary trust is set up in a will, the 'related settlements' will include any other trusts in the same will; for example, age-contingent gifts (see p 27). Instead, consider setting up a lifetime discretionary trust with nominal assets, known as a 'pilot trust', to which you can then make a gift in your will. This avoids setting up another trust on the same day as a discretionary trust and, of course, saves tax 10 years along the line.

There is also an 'exit charge', which applies when capital assets (as opposed to income) in the trust fund are given out to the beneficiaries and/or when the trust comes to an end. Broadly speaking, the rate exit charge is levied at a rate which is related to the 10-year charge – the nearer you are to the next 10th anniversary, the greater the proportion of the 10-year charge you have to pay.

You will by now have come to realise how very far a discretionary trust is from most people's idea of a tax haven. You can find yourself paying to go in, paying to get out, and having an expensive birthday every 10 years. Take professional advice before you try this at home!

Accumulation and maintenance (A & M) trusts

An accumulation and maintenance trust is a form of discretionary trust which enjoys favourable tax treatment (well, relatively favourable) as long as the beneficiaries are under 25 years of age. Like any discretionary trust, it works on the basis that none of the beneficiaries has the right to the income or capital of the trust fund – it's up to the trustees to decide who gets what and when. The trustees have the power to spend money on the beneficiaries according to their needs – this is the 'maintenance' side of the trust. Whatever income the trustees do not spend on 'maintenance', they must save in the trust – this is where the 'accumulation' comes in.

Accumulation and maintenance trusts are often set up by grandparents for their infant grandchildren. Many school fee plans are like this. The premiums count as 'gifts from income' and are therefore exempt from Inheritance Tax. The capital is held in an accumulation and maintenance trust and both the income and the capital can be used towards school fees when the time comes.

A gift in your will 'to my grandson Marmaduke on attaining the age of 18' will also operate as an accumulation and maintenance trust. Marmaduke does not have a right to the money until he turns 18, but in the meantime the trustees can use the fund for his benefit.

Inheritance Tax

We are explaining the Inheritance Tax on A & M trusts first, because the terms of the trust must comply with strict rules to qualify for favourable treatment. Here are the rules:

o The trust must be a discretionary one. No beneficiary can have the *right* to either income or capital unless and until the trustees give it to them.

o *But* the trustees must give each beneficiary their share of the trust fund (or the right to income from it) no later than their 25th birthday.

- In the meantime, the trustees can use the trust fund to 'maintain' the beneficiaries.

- The trustees must 'accumulate' (save up) any surplus income – although they can usually only accumulate for 21 years (see p 28).

- All the potential beneficiaries must be the grandchildren of a common grandparent (*common* in this context means shared, not naff). If one of the grandchildren dies before inheriting, their children, widow or widower can (if the trustees so decide) inherit in their place.

- If, unusually, the potential beneficiaries do not share a common grandparent, the trust cannot continue for more than 25 years. In any case (see above), accumulation must normally stop after 21 years.

If the trust complies with the rules, it enjoys the following Inheritance Tax advantages:

- Unlike other discretionary trusts, there will be no 10-year charge (see above).

- There will be no exit charges (see above).

- In the case of an A & M trust that you set up in your lifetime, the transfer of assets to the trust will be a **PET** (contrast transfers to other lifetime discretionary trusts, which are liable to Inheritance Tax at the lifetime rate of 20% on the amount of the gift that exceeds the nil rate band).

The rules are very strict, and you must comply with all of them: a pick and mix approach is not allowed. Unless you abide by the rules, your gift will not be a **PET** at all, but some sort of feral creature on which the lifetime rate of **Inheritance Tax** of 20% will be payable.

The fix is to include a clause in the trust document to the effect that the trustees' powers and duties can be exercised only in accordance with the relevant law, that is, section 71 of the Inheritance Tax Act 1984.

- A & M trusts set up in a will do not get any favourable tax treatment on your death. The trustees are non-exempt beneficiaries. The assets you give to the trustees in your will are liable to

Inheritance Tax at the death rate of 40%, subject, as always, to the nil rate band.

Capital Gains Tax

No CGT will be payable on setting up an A & M trust in your will.

A lifetime gift to an A & M trust, however, may be a taxable disposal for CGT purposes (see p 65 on CGT on lifetime gifts, and also the Inland Revenue Helpsheet IR295, available from the Revenue's website: www.inlandrevenue.gov.uk).

If the trustees sell assets at a profit, CGT may also be payable. The trustees' annual exemption (the amount of profit they are allowed to make on the sale without paying tax) is only half that of an individual – just £4,100 in 2004/05 instead of £8,200. Trustees have their own special rate of tax, known as the RAT (rate applicable to trusts) which in 2004/05 is 40%.

When trustees of an A & M trust decide to hand over capital assets to a beneficiary, the Revenue treat the decision as a disposal for CGT purposes. If the trustees continue to hold the capital on behalf of the beneficiary, the Revenue say that the trustees have made a 'deemed disposal'. 'Hold-over relief' may be available on the disposal (or deemed disposal) as long as the beneficiary is not already entitled to income from the trust fund.

Under the default **statutory** rules (the ones that apply unless you make up your own), a **beneficiary** of an A & M trust will become entitled to the *income* at age 18. If the capital is not given to the beneficiary when they become entitled to the income, 'hold-over relief' will not be available and the handing over of the capital will be a taxable disposal for CGT purposes.

Income Tax

While the trust fund is in the trustees' hands, the 40% RAT applies to income, although dividends are taxed at 32.5%. So far as the trustees do not accumulate income but spend it on maintaining the beneficiaries, for tax purposes the money becomes the income of the beneficiaries – with one important exception.

The parent trap: Where a *parent* sets up a lifetime A & M trust for their children, any income from the trust fund that they use to maintain the children while they are under 18 will be treated for tax purposes as the parent's income. As a result, the child's annual allowances will not be available and the income will be taxed at the highest rate applicable to the parent.

This does *not* apply to A & M trusts set up by the children's grandparents, godparents or doting aunts and uncles!

Trust for a person with a mental disability

This type of trust enjoys the most favourable tax treatment of all, and there are Inheritance Tax and CGT benefits. The slight snag is that the rules for the two taxes are not consistent. For further details, see p 173. In the 2004 Budget, the Government announced its intention to bring in new rules so that 'trusts set up for the most vulnerable are taxed as though the vulnerable person was receiving the income and gains directly, therefore ensuring that they enjoy the full benefit of their personal allowances and lower rate bands'.

Trusts for bankrupts and the irresponsible

There is a statutory framework for what are known as Protective Trusts (for further details, see p 35). In practice, it is common for people to use discretionary trusts instead of protective trusts, as the discretionary trust provides greater flexibility in responding to individual circumstances.

Modernising trusts

The Government says it wants to make trust taxation 'less burdensome' (so they say) for people not using trusts to avoid tax. In practice, they intend to introduce a basic rate band for trusts (which will be lower than the RAT). As a result, trusts with small incomes taxed at source will have no further tax liability and will not have to submit tax returns. Tax cuts are rare, however – so watch this space!

13

Funeral arrangements

You do not have to include your funeral arrangements in your will, and there may be good reasons not to do so.

o   If nobody reads your will until after your funeral, your wishes may be overlooked.

o   Your executors are not bound by your funeral instructions, and in fact they have the legal power to cremate your body whatever your stated preference (it is, of course, open to you to come back and haunt them).

o   The variety of funeral arrangements you can ask for (as opposed to those you are allowed to have and/or can afford!), is huge, but have a care – you should not lose sight of practicality and expense.

1   Don't wait until you are on your deathbed before mentioning funeral arrangements to your family.

Do not be shy about discussing this subject: make sure your family know your views – after all, it's *your* funeral!

2   Consumer rights apply to funerals too, and funeral directors, like any other service provider, should give good value for money. The Office of Fair Trading website www.oft.gov.uk offers some excellent leaflets under the generic title *Your Rights When Shopping* (!), including *Choosing a Funeral Director, Funeral Costs and Pre-paid Funerals*.

3   If, at the time of your death, you or your partner were receiving state benefits, your family may, in certain circumstances, be able to claim a grant from the Benefits Agency Social Fund to help with your funeral expenses. Ask your local CAB for details, or click on www.adviceguide.org.uk and type 'Funeral' in the Search box.

Pre-paid funerals

One way which may ensure your wishes are carried out is to arrange and pay for your funeral in advance. Many funeral directors offer this service. But:

o   Check what will happen if the funeral director goes out of business before you die. Do not subscribe to a scheme unless your advance payment is ring-fenced in a separate trust until your death.

o   If you intend to pay by instalments, check what will happen if you die before the final payment (you can usually take out payment protection insurance).

o   Check what will happen if you die out of the funeral director's area.

o   Make sure your family know about the arrangement, because there may not be a refund – keep a copy of the paperwork with your will.

Ask around your local funeral directors if this idea appeals to you. Or type 'pre-paid funeral' into an internet search engine if you'd like a thousand or more sites to choose from! The sensible alternative is to read the Office of Fair Trading factsheet on pre-paid funerals (click on www.oft.gov.uk/Consumer/Your+Rights+When+Shopping/Funerals+pre-paid). Visit the National Association of Funeral Directors website (www.nafd.org.uk) for details of suitable schemes in your area.

What kind of funeral?

Detailed advice on funeral arrangements is outside the scope of this book There is a bewildering amount of information on the web; keying in 'funeral arrangements' produces around 17,000 hits. We liked the Age Concern leaflet *Arranging a Funeral*, available at www.ace.org.uk/AgeConcern/information_307.htm.

Meanwhile, however, here are a few sources of inspiration.

Cremation

Cremation is the default option, in that your **executors** have a legal right to cremate your body whatever your stated preferences may be. Most crematoria are run by local authorities. You can find out more about cremation from the Cremation Society of Great Britain (website www.cremation.org.uk, full details in 'Useful contacts'). They publish two free booklets, *History of Modern Cremation* (written in 1974 on the occasion of the Cremation Society's Centenary) and *What You Should Know About Cremation*. Both are available online as well as by post – click on 'Journal and Publications' on their website.

Most religions allow cremation, except orthodox Judaism, Islam, Eastern Orthodox Christianity and a few Fundamentalist Christian faiths. Cremation is the usual method of disposal for Sikhs, Hindus and Buddhists. The Roman Catholic Church has accepted cremation since 1963 and Roman Catholic priests are allowed to conduct the cremation service at a crematorium. Also, the Cremation Society (details above) publish a booklet, *May Catholics Choose Cremation?*, price £4.50. If you have religious concerns about cremation, ask your priest, imam, etc for guidance.

Cremation now has the equivalent of the Royal Warrant! Traditionally, members of the British Royal Family choose to be buried, but Princess Margaret, who died in February 2002, was cremated at Slough Crematorium after a service at St George's Chapel, Windsor. Her ashes were placed in the Royal Vault in St George's Chapel.

Scattering ashes

Cremation produces between two and three kilograms (between five and seven pounds) of ashes, which are given to the next of kin in an urn. Many choose to scatter them in the crematorium's Garden of Remembrance and maybe plant a rose bush there, or pay for an entry in a Book of Remembrance.

If you want your ashes scattered on private land (including churchyards), whoever does the scattering will need the landowner's permission.

Burial

○ In theory, everyone has the right to be buried in the churchyard of the parish in which they die – provided there *is* a churchyard (many churchyards have been built over) and provided there is space (many churchyards are full). If there is space available in your local churchyard, you can usually reserve a plot in advance.

○ Cemeteries are usually run by local authorities and they too allow you to reserve a plot in advance.

1 A local council asked its new computer how much land would be needed for burials over the next 25 years. The answer was much lower than expected, so they checked the figures manually. The computer had, quite logically, decided the coffins should be buried vertically. Well, vertical burials are not unheard of. For centuries the tale was told that the poet Ben Jonson was buried in Westminster Abbey, standing up because he was too poor to afford a six-foot plot. In Victorian times, when a grave was being dug nearby, two leg bones were found standing upright, and a skull rolled down from above them. For more about vertical burials, access your favourite internet search engine, type 'buried standing up' and see what comes up.

2 In some countries, the overcrowding problem is solved by digging up bones after a prescribed time and stacking them in catacombs before recycling the graveyard plot. And why not?

○ Green burials, with biodegradable coffins and trees instead of gravestones, are growing in popularity. For information about green burials and a list of sites in your area, contact the Natural Death Centre on www.naturaldeath.org.uk. Their memorial website www.ifishoulddie.co.uk/alternative-burials.htm offers useful guidance on organising green burials as well as alternative and DIY burials.

○ Muslim burials require special facilities. The Leicester Muslim Burial Trust acts as a point of contact for Muslim funerals throughout the UK and offers a seven-day-a-week helpline (see 'Useful contacts').

Funerals – can you DIY?

Many grieving families prefer to hand over the funeral arrangements to a professional. A funeral director will take care of everything – at a price.

However, you do *not* need to engage professional funeral directors, and the saving if your family arrange a DIY funeral can be substantial. For further details, see the *New Natural Death Handbook* (£10.99, or £12.99 by mail order from the Natural Death Centre – details in 'Useful contacts'), which discusses everything from budget-price coffins to the ceremony itself. You can get more information by clicking on www.ukonline.gov.uk and typing 'funeral without a funeral director' in the Search box. Most of the sites come from local authorities, however, and the situation may not be the same in your area.

We enjoyed a piece in the *Guardian* entitled *The DIY Send-off*. Read it on: www.guardian.co.uk/consumer/story/0,3605,178177,00.html.

Burial on private land

You do not have to have your body buried in an official burial ground. The burial of Diana Princess of Wales in the grounds at Althorp drew attention to the idea of being buried at home. More mundanely, in June 2003 a *Times* reader announced her wish to be buried in her vegetable garden, saying 'Dead is dead, but I want my body to be of some use to Mother Nature'.

A single burial in your back garden (provided it is *your* garden – that is, you own the freehold – and not your landlord's) does not usually require official permission, but it *may* do so. The current legal position seems to be that a single burial in an unmarked grave (though an apple tree would not count as 'marking') does not require planning permission, but monumental masonry or fencing may do so, since they are forms of 'development'. But what about the next occupant of your house?

According to the 'If I should die' website, a burial in the garden might bring down the value of your home by as much as 25%. They add: 'It is also worth bearing in mind the possible emotional and practical difficulties presented by moving house. Once remains have been buried, they may not be disturbed or removed without authority. Your family will have to face leaving the grave behind or else apply for a Home Office licence for exhumation.'

Furthermore:

o Multiple burials on the same site may require planning permission for change of use of the land.

o Your burial should not disturb an archaeological site without permission.

o You may also require permission from the water authority if the burial threatens to pollute the water supply.

o You may also require the landowner's permission if you yourself do not own the site.

o If you die of a virulent disease, a burial on private land may be undesirable for reasons of public health or waste management.

o In some places, there are regulations about the depth of graves.

A simpler solution would be to ask for your body to be cremated and your ashes scattered in your garden instead.

Record keeping

After the burial, the date and place must be notified within 96 hours to the Registrar of Births, Marriages and Deaths on the form provided for the purpose.

To prevent surprises for future occupants of the property, we would also recommend that a plan showing the position of the grave should be placed with the title deeds of the property. The Land Registry does not require notification, however.

DIY cremation?

It depends what you mean by DIY ...

You can certainly arrange a cremation without using a funeral director, but you must use an official crematorium. Using a funeral pyre in the back garden is a criminal offence under the Cremation Act 1902.

William Price, a Welsh doctor and part time Druid, whimsically named his infant son Jesus Christ. The child died young, and Dr Price ritually burned the body on a funeral pyre. There was outrage in the valleys. Dr Price was prosecuted, only to be acquitted when it became apparent that he had not broken the law. The result was the Cremation Act 1902, which now regulates such activities and make it a criminal offence not to use an official crematorium.

There have been no open-air cremations in the UK since the 1940s, when the body of a Nepalese diplomat was cremated on a funeral pyre on private land in the south of England.

Burial at sea

The days are gone when the sailmaker sewed you up in canvas – putting the last stitch through your nose to make sure you were dead – and placed a cannon ball at your feet.

For burial at sea you now need a licence. This is issued free of charge by DEFRA – the Department of the Environment, Food and Rural Affairs. But that is the cheap, easy bit.

Burial at sea is now regulated to prevent bodies getting washed up on bathing beaches and getting caught in fishing nets.

The body must be free of infection, and must not have been embalmed. There are strict rules about the construction of the coffin. There are now only two places around the coast of England and Wales where sea burials are allowed. They are on the South Coast – one between Newhaven and Hastings and the other off the Needles, Isle of Wight. You can read all about it in *Burial*

at Sea – Instructions for Obtaining a Licence under the Food and Environment Protection Act 1985:
www.mceu.gov.uk/mceu_local/fepa/fepa-burial.htm.

No licence is needed for the scattering of cremation ashes at sea.

Ceremonies

Rosy recalls an old farmer whose funeral arrangements ran to a page and a half in his otherwise simple will. You probably have your own ideas about the kind of send-off you would like, and may even have chosen favourite music and prayers or poems. Princess Margaret chose the music and readings for her funeral in 2002, and everyone else has the right to do the same.

There are websites which suggest music and readings for funerals. We liked the general advice in *It's Your Funeral*, issued by the Funeral Standards Council on www.funeral-standards-council.co.uk.

It is usual, and often a great comfort to grieving families and friends, for someone who knew the dead person well to give a eulogy – literally, 'a good word', which has come to mean a funeral address in praise of the dead person. This might seem a daunting task, but there is a free booklet available online at www.funeralcare.co-op.co.uk/well_chosen_words.asp or from any Co-op funeral home – call 0800 0686 727 for details of one near you. The booklet, entitled *Well Chosen Words*, has a foreword by the Poet Laureate, Andrew Motion, and is a step-by-step guide to writing a eulogy.

We also liked Stewarton Bible School, Scotland http://atschool.eduweb.co.uk/sbs777, a resolutely Christian site which suggests a framework for the ceremony, music, Bible readings and ideas for the eulogy. Other faiths are catered for on the web too, and a little surfing will show you.

A religious ceremony is not the only option. For information about non-religious ceremonies, contact the British Humanist Association. They offer a free factsheet online at www.humanism.org.uk and will supply a list of people in your area who can conduct non-religious ceremonies. They also publish a booklet called *Funerals Without God*, £4.50 (see 'Useful contacts').

Not all priests are happy to conduct Christian funerals for gay people. Call the Lesbian and Gay Christian Movement for a list of priests who are happy to do so (see 'Useful contacts').

Medical use of your body after death

In his will, the philosopher, lawyer and reformer Jeremy Bentham donated his body to his friend Doctor Southwood Smith, who was to put the soft parts in labelled glass cases and articulate the skeleton 'in such a manner that the whole figure may be seated in a chair usually occupied by me when living'. Dressed in one of Bentham's own black suits, the skeleton was to preside over meetings of his 'personal friends and other disciples'. Bentham's body can still be seen in the South Cloisters of University College London.

Not many people would want to follow Bentham's example, but you might wish your body to help someone after you die. There are three ways in which you can do this:

o   donation of 'organs' and 'tissues' (see below for an explanation) for transplant purposes;

o   donation of tissue for research purposes;

o   donation of your entire body for teaching and/or research.

Since the abolition of slavery, it has not been possible in law for anyone to own a live human body – not even your own body, although you do have control over what happens to it in your lifetime. After your death, the law talks not of ownership but of 'lawful possession'. The right to 'lawful possession' gives the right to decide what (within the law) happens to the body.

If there is doubt about the cause of your death, the coroner will have the right to 'lawful possession' of your body for whatever time they need in order to establish why you died. Newspaper reports of deaths in suspicious circumstances often talk of the coroner 'releasing the body to the family'. In fact, the coroner must release the body to the next in line. If you have made a will in which you have appointed executors, they will have the right to 'lawful possession' of your body. Failing that, your next of kin will be next in line! Broadly speaking, the 'next of kin' will be entitled to 'lawful possession' of the body in the same order as in the **intestacy** rules (see pp 4–5). Under current law, this means that unmarried partners of either sex do not have rights to your body in circumstances where you have not appointed them as your executors – another reason for making a will! In practice, of course, the people with the right to 'lawful possession' of your body will prefer to leave it in the *actual* possession of the undertaker.

The position, therefore, is that whoever has the right to 'lawful possession' of your body can choose:

o   to have your body cremated, whatever wishes you have expressed to the contrary; and

o   to refuse consent for your body to be used for organ donation, teaching or research, despite whatever wishes you have expressed in your lifetime.

Be quite clear, therefore, that despite any requests you make, the final decision about what happens to your body is out of your control. You can register with a donor scheme and make your wishes known – but those with the right to 'lawful possession' of your body have the final choice.

Three different statutes provide the legal framework for the donation of organs, tissue and whole bodies:

o   The Human Organ Transplants Act 1989 governs the use of donated organs for transplant purposes.

o   The Human Tissue Act 1961 provides for the use of human tissue for research as opposed to transplant or teaching.

o   When people donate their bodies to be dissected for teaching purposes, the Anatomy Acts (the earliest was passed in 1832, the most recent in 1984) apply.

Donating 'organs' and 'tissues' for transplant

Many bodies that are buried or cremated could have been used to save lives if only the person had made their wishes known in their lifetime. You can choose to donate any part of your body that the doctors have a use for, or specify particular organs. At the time of writing, 11,030,268 people had already signed up with the NHS Organ Donor Register.

What is an organ? The Human Organ Transplants Act defines an organ as 'any part of a human body consisting of a structured arrangement of tissues which, if wholly removed, cannot be replicated by the body'. However, in their information documents, the Department of Health on their transplant site www.uktransplant.org.uk talks about 'organs' – which must be transplanted 'fresh', and 'tissues' – which can be frozen, stored and transplanted when needed. We are keeping the inverted commas here to preserve this distinction.

'Organs' which are transplanted in the UK are:

o   heart
o   lung
o   liver
o   kidney
o   pancreas
o   small intestine.

'Tissues' for transplant include:

o   cornea
o   skin
o   bone
o   heart valves
o   tendons
o   ligaments.

Not everyone who dies will be a potential 'organ' donor – the doctors are looking for low-mileage hearts, lungs, etc in excellent condition – but nearly everyone can donate corneas, bone, skin and other 'tissues'. Those that are not suitable for transplant purposes may still be used for research – see 'Tissue for medical research' below.

At the time of writing, over 5,800 people were waiting for 'organ' transplants. There have been calls for a new law to treat all adults as potential donors unless they have expressly stated otherwise.

For 'organ' donation for transplant purposes, time is of the essence. The 'organs' must be removed immediately after 'brain stem death', with machines keeping the blood circulating.

'Organs' like hearts and kidneys get all the publicity, but 'tissues' like corneas, bone and skin are important too. Your cornea could restore someone's sight. Bone and tendons are used for reconstruction after an injury and a bone transplant can save someone with bone cancer from losing a limb. Heart valves are used to help children and adults with diseased or damaged hearts, while skin grafts can save the lives of people with severe burns.

There is a national framework of clinical 'tissue' banks, co-ordinated by Regional Tissue Services Divisions of the United Kingdom Transplant Programme provided through the National Blood Service. These tissue banks retrieve tissue, mainly from orthopaedic surgery and what they call 'cadaveric referral' and we'd call donated bodies (see below), and store it until it is needed.

Registration as an organ donor enables the medical teams to make use of any part of your body that you do not explicitly exclude, so even if your heart or kidneys are useless for transplanting, your gift could still improve several people's lives.

Nobody ought to make a decision like this on the spur of the moment (but see 'Deathbed donations', p 125). There is a lot of helpful information available online. Try www.nhs.uk/nhsupdate/be_an_organ_donor.asp which has links to the NHS Organ Donor website and several others. See also *Organ Donation – Your Questions Answered* on www.uktransplant.org.uk.

See 'Useful contacts' for more websites about organ donation and transplantation.

If, having read up on the subject, you decide to donate your 'organs' (and that includes 'tissues' like corneas too

– see above) for transplant purposes, the next step is to get onto the NHS Organ Donor Register. This is a nationwide, confidential list of people willing to be organ donors after their death.

There is a national, computerised list of people waiting for organ transplants. The NHS Organ Donor Register helps to match patients to donors quickly. It also makes it easier for your family to accept organ donation when they know you have made the effort to register.

Interestingly, children under 16 can be donors if they have expressed a wish and their parent or guardian agrees to donation.

Registration of your intention to be a donor is not actually obligatory – just carrying a donor card makes your wishes known – but it is important to register, because:

o   donor cards can get lost;

o   you might not be carrying yours at the crucial moment.

You can register using any of the following methods:

o   Pick the form up at any chemist shop or doctor's surgery, fill it in and post it off.

o   On applying for a driving licence or passport, or registering with a new GP.

o   Call the Organ Donation line on 0845 6060 400 – lines are open 7 am to 11 pm seven days a week – and ask for a copy of their leaflet *Join the NHS Organ Donor Register and Give the Gift of Life*, which contains a registration form.

o   Write, free of charge, to:
     The NHS Organ Donor Register
     PO Box 14
     FREEPOST
     Patchway
     Bristol
     BS34 8ZZ

o   Online. Access: www.gift-of-life.org.uk/donor_register. This site is run by the Gift of Life Commemorative Trust. Alternatively, access the UK Transplant website on www.uktransplant.org.uk/odronline/servlet/myd etailsservlet and register. Both take just a few moments to complete.

When you complete the registration form online, you are asked for email details of anyone who needs to know you have registered.

o Sign up for certain credit and loyalty cards. For example, anyone who applies for the Boots loyalty card can join the Organ Donor Register by simply ticking a box on the application form.

o On applying for a driving licence – just tick the organ donation box and your name is added to the register automatically.

1 Please let your family and friends know! Your body will be past its sell-by date by the time anyone reads such intentions in your will. *Organ Donation – Your Questions Answered* on www.uktransplant. org uk suggests ways of raising the subject with your family. Moreover, we repeat that, strictly speaking, the final decision is up to 'the person lawfully in possession of the body after death' – in practice, your executors or, if you do not appoint any, your next of kin. However, the Transplant Service says 'Objection is almost unknown if the family is aware that their relative wished to donate'.

2 It isn't only transplant surgery that requires human tissue (see 'Tissue for medical research' below).

Tissue for medical research

If you want your body to be used for medical research rather than for students to dissect (see below), this too is possible, although it is more of a loan than a donation (see below).

Human tissue is always needed for medical research. If you feel strongly about experiments on live animals, you will be pleased to know that human tissue is widely used for medical research, including the testing of drugs. The Tissue Bank (see below) says, 'Many treatments and medications react differently in animal models than when they are used clinically in humans. Consequently, human tissue is a more appropriate model in which to study human disease'.

The Tissue Bank website www.tissuebank.co.uk/uses explains how human tissue can help to develop effective, safe drugs to fight diseases such as cancer, multiple sclerosis, leukaemia, heart disease, AIDS, Alzheimer's, muscular dystrophy and diabetes ... and at the same time reduce the number of animals sacrificed in the search of cures for human diseases.

Although organs such as hearts and kidneys cannot be used for transplanting unless they are in good shape, almost everyone can donate tissue, however old and worn-out their major organs may be.

Peterborough District Hospital's Human Research Tissue Bank has set up a Tissue Donation After Death Register for people who want to donate their tissue for research, as opposed to their organs for transplant.

You can read about the scheme on www.tissuebank.co.uk/body and print out a two-part consent form from www.tissuebank.co.uk/pmdec.

The form sets out the conditions quite clearly:

o   all donated tissue becomes anonymous;

o   tissue is not sold, but costs are recovered on a non profit making basis;

o   any tissue which remains unused after 10 years will be disposed of in a lawful manner;

o   neither the donor nor the Tissue Bank will benefit financially if the research leads to a new treatment or medical test;

o   relevant medical information may be recorded and held on a database and supplied anonymously to the relevant research company.

With the form comes a Details Form on which you fill in your details and also those of your GP and your next of kin.

If you accept the terms, you should sign your form and send it to:

> Tissue Bank Administrator
> Histology Department
> Peterborough District Hospital
> Thorpe Road
> Peterborough
> PE3 6DA

They will then send you a laminated donor card with the hospital's details. We repeat: your choice to donate your tissue is not binding on those with the right to 'lawful possession' of your body, who can override your wishes.

As with organ donation, time is of the essence, so it is important to register with the scheme during your lifetime. You should also let your family and your GP know your intentions immediately (see the 'Power point' about organ transplant above). Moreover, the final decision about releasing your body for research rests with 'the person lawfully in possession of the body after death' – in practice your executors or, if you have none, your next of kin.

The Department will collect bodies from within a 150-mile radius but they will register details of anyone in the UK, as they hope other hospitals will follow suit and the Peterborough team will then be able to pass on details of donors in their areas. Bodies are kept for just 24 hours, after which they are returned to the family for the funeral arrangements of their choice.

Donating your body for medical teaching

Each year about 800 bodies are donated and used to help train doctors, nurses and dentists. WA Harris, Professor of Anatomy at Cambridge University, said in 2001:

> The study of anatomy ... helps to lay the foundations for all future ... medical practice ... We recognise that the donation of a body may be a person's last act of benevolence reflecting a life of generosity, for which we are enormously grateful.

'Burke's the butcher, Hare's the thief,
Knox the man who buys the beef.'

Before the 1832 Anatomy Act it was only lawful to dissect the corpses of executed murderers, so there was a dire shortage of bodies for anatomy classes. It was the scandal of Burke and Hare, who supplied fresh cadavers to Doctor Knox for his anatomy classes, that led to the Act, which legalised the use of 'unclaimed' corpses. This in practice meant they could now be bought from workhouses instead of cut down from scaffolds, snatched from graveyards or – in the case of Burke and Hare – lured to Hare's lodging house, plied with whisky and suffocated.

Bodies are usually given to the medical school nearest the person's home. This is because university anatomy departments have a 'catchment area' for donated bodies. For example, Cambridge accepts bodies from East Anglia, and Manchester and Bristol both enforce a 25 mile radius.

To donate your body for teaching purposes, there are three stages:

1   Find out the name and address of your nearest medical school. To do this, approach the London Anatomy Office (if you live in the London area) on 0208 846 1216 or HM Inspector of Anatomy on 0207 972 4342 – full details in 'Useful contacts'.

2   Complete a form of request that your body be used for teaching purposes. The medical school you have approached will usually send you an explanatory leaflet and their own form of request or authorisation. Otherwise use the sample form on p 145. The request/authorisation form will usually allow you to choose:

    o   whether the medical school may retain organs after dissection;

    o   whether you would like your body to be buried or cremated when they have finished with it.

3   Make sure that your **executors** and family know the form exists. (If the medical school want you to return the form to them, keep a copy for your executors and family.) This is because the final decision rests with 'the person lawfully in possession of the body after death' – in practice, your executors or next of kin.

When you die, your executors (or next of kin if you have not appointed executors) should notify the medical school as soon as possible so that they can decide whether they can accept your body. Your family must also notify the local Registrar of Births, Marriages and Deaths and obtain a Certificate for Burial or Cremation.

Then, if they accept your body, the medical school will send an undertaker (usually at their expense) to collect your body and the certificate.

There is no guarantee that your body will be accepted. Medical schools prefer bodies that are within easy collecting distance (see above). Age does not matter, but the following disorders will usually disqualify a body:

o   post mortem examination;

o   removal of major organs for transplant purposes;

o   an amputated limb;

o   extensive surgery;

o   obesity or emaciation;

o   a history of cancer;

o   Alzheimer's Disease and some other neurological disorders;

o   tuberculosis;

o   hepatitis;

o   gangrene;

o   HIV/AIDS.

You will see from this list of 'disqualifications' that you cannot have it every which way – you cannot donate your organs for transplant *and* your body for tissue research *and* your body for medical examination. What you can do, however, is leave a request to your family that in the event of your organs not being removed for transplant for whatever reason, you wish your body to be donated for medical examination.

Bear in mind that once the medical school have your body, it comes under their control, with no conditions attached other than your choice of eventual burial or cremation.

After they have collected your body, there is usually no further communication between the medical school and your family and/or executors unless, at the time you make your donation, you ask for your ashes to be returned to your family.

Do bear in mind that if you donate your body for students to learn on, the medical school may need it for a long time. The legal maximum is three years. This will of course have implications for your funeral, due to the absence of a body. One answer is a service of thanksgiving or a 'celebration of life' shortly after your death.

A small group of students will be taught using the same body for the whole teaching year. At Cambridge there is a non-denominational committal service within the Anatomy Department. At this service the students and staff give thanks to those who have generously given their bodies to train the next generation of doctors. Professor Harris says: 'For the first time, during the committal Service, the students learn the name of the person they have studied. This is important for our students and they are given time in which to say a personal and private "thank you".'

At some other medical schools, donors' families may be invited to the service: practices vary.

You can find out more about this subject in the Department of Health's paper *The Removal, Retention and Use of Human Organs and Tissue from Post-Mortem Examination*. Don't let the title put you off – it deals with donation of bodies for anatomical examination too. Click on www.doh.gov.uk/tissue.

Deathbed donations

However you wish your body to be used, whether for organ transplants, tissue for medical research or your whole body for teaching, the same provision for last-minute bequests applies. While it is clearly better to do this in writing, a spoken request during your last illness is sufficient, provided you make your request in front of two witnesses.

Interlude – living wills and enduring powers of attorney

As before, your executors or next of kin can override your request. Consider haunting them if they do …

We call this an interlude because, strictly speaking, it does not deal with your **will** in the sense (see

'Buzzwords') of 'a document in which you say what you wish to happen to your money and property when you die, and who should carry out your wishes'.

You might say, however, that the two documents we are about to discuss are linked with will-making because, like a will, they involve foresight and planning for the future. To make a **living will**, or to give someone you trust an **enduring power of attorney**, is to acknowledge that:

o   you are mortal; *and*

o   your intellect may one day be impaired.

Such an acknowledgment does not, however, imply helplessness or inadequacy – on the contrary, you will, while you are still 'captain of your soul', be making legally binding arrangements for your wishes to be carried out if, in the future, you become unable either to make your own decisions or to communicate them to others. In particular:

o   both a living will and an enduring power of attorney provide for your wishes to be carried out in circumstances where you would otherwise be helpless;

o   both can, one hopes, spare those you love from doubt, anxiety and guilt.

Living wills

All sick people are entitled to refuse medical treatment, and a doctor who persists in treating patients against their express instructions may be guilty of criminal assault. But what happens if you are incurably ill but no longer have the mental capacity to refuse treatment? The answer is to make your wishes known beforehand. An advance request of this kind is called, variously, a living will, an advance request, an advance directive, or an advance refusal (of treatment).

A living will, therefore, is not really a will at all. It is an advance refusal of medical treatment, *but not basic care*, which you intend to have effect if and when:

o   you lack the physical capacity to communicate your refusal; *or*

o   you lack the **mental capacity** to refuse treatment; and in either case o   your quality of life is very poor; *and*

o   there is no hope of recovery or even significant improvement.

A living will does not yet have **statutory** force (although, at the time of writing, the Draft Mental Incapacity Bill proposes to change this). All the same, the courts have in recent years determined that a living will, made in advance, that expresses your wishes clearly and is applicable to your case, will be as effective as any request you made when you were ill. Additionally, the British Medical Association advises doctors that they are legally obliged to comply with such advance requests.

Living Wills and Enduring Powers of Attorney, in the *Pocket Lawyer* series, offers more information and you can download our Living Will from the website.

If you make a living will, you must make sure that everyone who needs to know about it has a copy. These people are likely to include:

o   family members;

o   your doctor;

o   your carer (if applicable);

o   the hospital looking after you (if applicable).

Enduring Power of Attorney (EPA) – handing over the reins

Most of us hope to die at a ripe old age in full possession of our faculties. Be realistic, however. If you are over 70 or in poor health, you should consider arranging for your affairs to be looked after by someone else if you become unable to deal with things for yourself.

The simplest way to do this is to make what is called an **Enduring Power of Attorney**, EPA for short. There is a special form for this – nothing else will do. An EPA gives the person of your choice – your attorney – the right to take over the running of your affairs in such circumstances. Otherwise, a person not of your choice – an official from the **Public Guardianship Office** of the **Court of Protection** – will take over.

As soon as your attorney believes that you can no longer cope mentally, they have a duty to register your EPA with the Public Guardianship Office. The effect of registration is to give your attorney the power to continue to handle your affairs.

Granting an EPA does not mean handing over control while you are still mentally alert, however. You can give someone an EPA on the understanding that they will not exercise their power while you are still able to cope. You can, in fact, state specifically on your EPA form that the power will not come into force until the attorneys actually apply to the Court of Protection for the EPA to be registered. Also, as long as you have the mental capacity to do so, you can cancel an EPA at any time.

The choice of attorney is crucial. Broadly speaking, you would look for the same qualities in an attorney as you would in an executor, and in practice it is often sensible to grant an EPA to someone you have also chosen to be your executor. This will also ensure a seamless transition when you die. At your death, your attorney's authority ends and your executor's authority begins. Note that the Public Guardianship Office believes there is a high level of abuse of EPAs by attorneys, using them to plunder the assets of vulnerable people. A new Mental Incapacity Act (it is in draft form at the time of writing) will replace the existing EPA system with one that is less open to abuse (details of the Public Guardianship Office are in 'Useful contacts').

You can read more about EPAs in *Living Wills and Enduring Powers of Attorney* in this series.

Have you got it all together?

Your will itself is only part of what you need to ensure that your **assets** go the people you want. Here is a checklist of loose ends that you may need to tie up.

❏ **Joint property** – remember, if you want to leave your share to someone in your will, you can only do so if 'the rule of survivorship' does not apply. If appropriate, keep a copy of the notice to disapply the rule of survivorship with your will.

❏ **Death in service benefit** – if you die while in employment, there may be a lump sum available from your pension fund. This payment is often discretionary, that is, it is up to the trustees of your pension fund to decide how much to pay, and to whom. However, they will take your expressed wishes into account – as long as, of course, they are aware of your wishes! Ask your employers for the contact details of the trustees and tell them who you would like to benefit (see p 15 for fuller details).

❏ **Pensions** – if you are married, your widow/ widower will often receive a proportion of your pension after your death. Note that if you are estranged from your spouse but not fully divorced, you cannot nominate anyone else to receive your pension benefits. If you are unmarried, your partner will not automatically receive any benefits, but you can often nominate them. Note that at the time of writing, legislation is planned which will give same-sex couples the same rights (including pension rights) as heterosexual married couples.

Contact the pension fund trustees to make your wishes clear.

☐ Life **insurance policies** – see p 14 on policies written in trust. The advantage of this type of policy is that the proceeds do not form part of your estate and are paid direct to the person you name in the trust deed that is attached to the policy. Have you done this?

☐ **Organ donation** – have you registered with the NHS Organ Donor scheme and do you carry a donor card?

☐ **Tissue donation** – have you registered with the Tissue Bank, have you obtained a donor card and have you told your family?

☐ **Body donation** for medical teaching – have you filled in an authorisation form?

☐ **List of assets** – if no one knows about them, your beneficiaries may never inherit. Put the list with your will.

Finally, *destroy* any previous will.

Make things easy for your executors

It is distressing for bereaved families to have to rummage through reams of documents, which may be tucked away in some surprising places, for the information they need. It is helpful if you can make a note of the many details that your executors may require immediately after your death. We have listed these below. You can download, amend and print it at www.cavendishpublishing.com/pocketlawyer.

We have tried to put all the information your executors are likely to need into a single document. You can, of course, delete any item on the list that does not apply to your circumstances; for example, you would not have both the title deeds of your home and your tenancy agreement, and you may not have an employer.

As a lot of the information in this document is confidential, we suggest you give the document to whoever is going to act as your executor and ask them to keep it in a safe place. Keep a copy for yourself, together with all the other items mentioned in the list, in one accessible place.

Instructions for my Executors

Personal details

My name ....

My former name(s) (if any) ....

[Note that this could be important if, for example, as a woman you own assets in your maiden name – if applicable, identify which assets are in which name]

Address ....

....

Postcode ....

Telephone nos:

Home ....

Work ....

Fax no ....

email ....

Computer password(s) ....

....

National Insurance no ....

Organ donation – transplant

[We have put this section first, because it is time-critical. If you have not made any arrangements to donate your organs, delete this section]

My details are/are not registered with

The NHS Organ Donor Register
PO Box 14
FREEPOST
Patchway
Bristol
BS34 8ZZ
Tel 0845 60 60 400   YES/NO

You can find my organ donor card *(say where if applicable)*

....

Tissue donation – drug research

[If you have not made any arrangements to donate your tissue, delete this section]

My details are/are not registered with

Department of Histology
Peterborough District Hospital
Thorpe Road
Peterborough PE3 6DA
Tel 01733 874000

You can find my tissue donor card ....…......…..............
(say where if applicable)

Body donation for teaching purposes

[If you have not made any arrangements to donate your body, delete this section]

I have/have not arranged to donate my body to ....
....
(name and other details of the school of anatomy)

A copy of the form of authorisation is enclosed with my will
(see below). *(delete if this does not apply)*

Where to find things

[Delete anything that does not apply to you]

- keys (house, car, safe, etc) ....
- Will (dated ....) ....
- birth certificate ....
- marriage certificate ....
- medical card ....
- my list of assets ....
- insurance policies: ....
- buildings ....
- contents ....
- life ....
- other ....
- pension documents ....
- title deeds to any property ....
  *(or details of where these are
  kept, eg solicitor or bank)*
- tenancy agreement and rent book ....

- HP and loan agreements ....
- credit card and store card details . ...
- building society and bank details, including account numbers ....
- Post Office savings account books ....
- copies of tax returns, etc ....
- passport ....
- receipts and guarantees for major purchases ....
- savings and investment certificates ....
- vehicle registration documents and insurance details ....
- Premium Bond certificates ....
- Items on loan to me ....
  (eg equipment from local authorities or the Red Cross)
- *details of any liabilities which* ....
  may not be immediately ....
  obvious to your executors, ...
  such as guarantees given for ....
  the debts of a company ....
  or individual ....
- address book *(to inform* ....
  friends and relations)

People and organisations to inform

- Doctor

  Name ....
  Address ....
  Tel no ....
  email ....

- Solicitor

  Name ....
  Address ....
  Tel no ....
  email ....

- Bank

  Name ....

  Address ....

  Tel no ....

  email ....

  Current account no(s) ....

  Deposit account no(s) ....

  Items in safe custody ....

- Building Society

  Name ....

  Address ....

  Tel no ....

  email ....

  Account nos ....

- Employer

  Name ....

  Address ....

  Tel no ....

  email ....

  Ask whether any death in service benefit, etc will be payable

- Accountant

  Name ....

  Address ....

  Tel no ....

  email ....

- Insurance broker

  Name ....

  Address ....

  Tel no ....

  email ....

- Landlord

  Name ....

  Address ....

  Tel no ....

  email ....

- Priest/minister/rabbi, etc

  Name ....
  Address ....
  Tel no ....
  email ....

- Inspector of Taxes

  Name ....
  Address ....
  Tel no ....
  Reference no ....
  email ....

- Council *(regarding Council tax etc)*

  Name ....
  Address ....
  Tel no ....
  Reference no ....
  email ....

- Department for Work and Pensions

  Address ....
  Tel no ....
  email ....
  (only if you have been receiving State benefits)

- Utilities
  (such as water, electricity and gas companies)

- Clubs, trade unions, learned societies or professional associations

- Friends and relations

[Here you can list the names, addresses, email details and telephone numbers of your closest friends and relations, with a request for someone to go through your address book/database on your PC and inform the rest]

[Now add any other people or organisations who ought to be informed]

Keep your address book up to date! Most people's contain far too many obsolete entries.

Funeral Arrangements

[Here you can either refer your executors to your will for your wishes about funeral arrangements (see Chapter 13 for inspiration), or use the form below]

The funeral director I would prefer is

Name ....
Address ....
Tel no ....

Pre-Paid Funeral

(either)

I have a pre-paid funeral plan. On my death, please contact:

Organisation ....
Address ....
Tel no ....

(or)

I do not have a pre-paid funeral plan.

Burial/Cremation

(Now choose the option you want)

I wish to be buried at ....
I have reserved a burial plot with ....
at ....
Contact tel no .... *(use this if you have reserved a plot in a churchyard or cemetery)*

Or

I wish to be cremated.

(Here you add any directions about the disposal of the ashes)

Funeral Ceremony

[Here you add any directions about

- *the funeral ceremony;*
- *readings and/or music;*
- *flowers;*
- *donations to charity instead of flowers;*
- *memorials]*

Odds and ends

This chapter contains all the extra documents and clauses you are likely to need.

Joint property – tying up the loose ends

Earlier on, we mentioned the rule of survivorship.

If you do *not* want the rule of survivorship to apply, you must sign a document saying so. We print one below.

You can also, of course, download as many copies as you wish from our website. You need to complete it, then you *must* give copies to the other co-owner(s) of the property. Where the **asset** is **real estate**, you should also send a copy of your notice to the Land Registry.

It is also helpful to put a copy of the document in the envelope with your will.

The Land Registry is the Domesday Book for the 21st century. Most homes will have 'titles' (details of who owns them) registered at the Land Registry. If you can also notify the Land Registry that you have severed the joint tenancy, they will put what is called a 'restriction' on their register, so that the surviving co-owner(s) can't sell the property and walk off with the entire proceeds.

You can find details of your local Land Registry by accessing their website on www.landreg.gov.uk.

---

o   Here is the Notice you should use. For each co-owner make one copy *without* the extra wording and one *with* the extra wording.

- Send or hand each co-owner the original notice plus a copy, and ask them to confirm that they have received it by signing and dating the second copy only (see below).
- Each co-owner should then give or send the second copy back for you to keep.
- Keep your copy/copies with your will and other papers (see 'Make things easy for your executors', p 130).

Joint Property – Notice to Disapply Rule of Survivorship

From: *(your name and address)*

To: *(co-owner's name and address)*

Property: *(identify co-owned property, preferably with full address, postcode and, if possible, Land Registry title number, which should be on your deeds)*

I give you notice that from today the rule of survivorship is not to apply to the above property, and that it is now owned between us as beneficial tenants in common in the following shares:

My share ( ) %

Your share ( )%

Signed ....

Dated ....

(add this extra wording to the second copy)

I acknowledge receipt of the original notice, of which this is a copy.

Signed ....

Dated ....

Section 21 Statement

We explained about this on p 19. You make a Section 21 Statement if you want to exclude someone from your will who you think would then be able to make an Inheritance Act claim. Here is a standard Section 21 Statement. When you have signed and dated it, put it in a safe place with your will and other papers.

Section 21 Statement

I (*your name* ....)
Of (*your address* ....)
make the following statement setting out the reasons under
s 21 of the Inheritance (Provision for Family and Dependants)
Act 1975, why I have prepared a Will dated (*date* ....)
and not made provision for (*name* ....) as
follows:

'I have made my Will excluding (*name* ....)
because ....
....
....
....
....'

Extra clauses

These extra clauses are to our basic wills what the sprig of parsley or cherry tomato is to a restaurant meal.

Specific legacies

Examples of specific legacies might be £1,000, a piece of jewellery or a car. There are some traps with this type of legacy.

1   In the case of a gift other than money, is the description in your will sufficient to identify the **asset**?

2   Will you still own the same asset when you die? If you do not, the gift will lapse unless you describe your gift by reference to the category of asset that you own when you die. An example is 'the car which I own at the time of my death'. Our term for this is a 'gift of a mutable asset' (if it seems pompous to you, try thinking of something better).

Even then, the gift may still lapse if by the time you die you do not own anything in that category.

3   If you own – or may own at the time of your death – more than one diamond necklace/car/boat, how will your executors know which one you have in mind?

4   Are you sure the item is yours to leave (that is, not on hire purchase, etc)?

5   If you are rich enough to have to pay **Inheritance Tax**, will the person who gets the asset have to pay Inheritance Tax on it?

Here are some sample 'specific legacy' clauses.

Gift of Fixed Amount of Money

I give to (*name*) of (*address*) (£ ......) (free of Inheritance Tax).

Gift of Specific Asset

I give to (*name*) of (*address*) (free of Inheritance Tax) my (*describe item fully*).

Gift of Mutable Asset

I give to (*name*) of (*address*) the (*say what it is*) which I own at the time of my death (free of Inheritance Tax).

'Mutable' comes from the Latin *mutare* – to change. We coined this term ourselves because some assets – such as houses and cars – are, like mutant monsters from outer space, subject to change. The reason for adding 'which I own at the time of my death' is that the Morris Minor you own now may have mutated into an Aston Martin by the time you die.

Substitutional gift

Suppose you leave a gift to someone, but they die before you? In the case of a specific gift, the money or goods will go back into the general pot – unless you provide in your will for the gift to pass to someone else in substitution. This is a substitutional gift. An example would be as follows:

> I give free of taxes (*say what you are giving*) to (*name and address*) but if he/she dies before me I give this to (*name and address*).

For examples of substitutional gifts of residue, see Wills 3 and 4.

Substitute Executor

> I appoint (*Bilbo Baggins of Bag End, Hobbiton, the Shire*) as my Executor, but if he is unable or unwilling to act I appoint (*Frodo Baggins of Bag End, Hobbiton, The Shire*) in his place.

Children – receipt for gift

You can leave gifts to children under 18, but they cannot give your executors a valid receipt because they are still minors in the eyes of the law. This means that the executors cannot safely hand over the gift unless the will provides for someone else to give the receipt. Here is a clause with a gift to grandchildren, with provision for a receipt.

> I give (£ ....) free of Inheritance Tax to each of my grandchildren living at the date of my death. In the case of a grandchild under 18 the grandchild's parent or guardian can give a valid receipt to my executors.

Children – a clean slate

You may have made gifts to your children during your lifetime. Do you want these gifts to affect what they get under your will?

If you do, adjust your children's shares accordingly when you make your will – that is, leave less to the child who has already had a cut (see the explanation of **hotchpot**, p xv).

If you don't wish to do this, add a clause as follows:

> In ascertaining the entitlement of each of my children under my will, no account is to be taken of previous gifts made by me or by their other parent.

Will made in anticipation of marriage

> I am expecting to marry (*insert name*) (`my intended'). My Will is to have immediate effect, and is not to be revoked by my marriage to my intended.

Signature clause for blind testator

> Date:
>
> Signature of (*insert person's name*) signing on my behalf
>
> ....
>
> As I am blind, my Will has been read aloud to me. I understand and approve it. I have authorised *(insert person's name)* to give effect to my Will by signing it in my presence and in the presence of the two witnesses named below; and both of them have signed it in our presence.
>
> | | Witness 1 | Witness 2 |
> |---|---|---|
> | Signature: | .... | |
> | Full name: | .... | |
> | Address: | .... | |
> | Occupation: | .... | |

The 30-day clause

> On condition that (*insert your spouse or partner's full name*) survives me by 30 days, I give the whole of my estate to (*insert your spouse or partner's full name*) and appoint (*insert your spouse or partner's full name*) as my sole executor.

[Of course, if you use the 30-day clause, you really must set out what will happen to your estate if you outlive your partner, or they die within 30 days of your death.]

Funeral arrangements

Remember (see p 105), your wishes are not binding on your executors. All the same, many people derive great comfort from planning their funerals, including the music to be played and a lavish wake for the mourners. See Chapter 13 for inspiration.

A wake was originally an all-night watch over a corpse, during which the mourners would take turns to pray over the body by candlelight and protect it from body snatchers. This vigil was followed by feasting after the funeral. At modern wakes the vigil is optional but the feasting is still popular.

You need not go into detail in your will, especially if you have left instructions elsewhere (see our suggestions on p 130).

Here are some typical clauses:

- I should like my body to be cremated.
- I should like my body to be buried at *[be specific and check that space is available. In some churchyards and cemeteries you can pay in advance to reserve a plot]*.
- I should like my body to be buried next to my late husband/wife *[name]*. *[Be specific here, especially if you have been married more than once!]*
- No flowers, please; instead, donations may be made to *[name and number of charity]*.
- I would like a green burial with a tree on my grave as a memorial. If my executors do not know how to arrange this, or the location of the nearest suitable site, they can find out from an organisation such as the Natural Death Centre, tel no 0207 359 8301.

Or indeed you could delegate the whole thing to your executors:

- I should like my executors to make such funeral arrangements as they think appropriate.

Organ donation

Your will is not the place to raise this issue for the first time. Here, however, is a clause to include in your will:

I wish to donate all or any of my organs for transplant or other medical purposes, if required. If the hospital removes organs but does not make use of them, it may retain or destroy them at its discretion.

Donating your body for medical teaching

This again is something that, if possible, you should arrange in your lifetime, as it is helpful to establish in advance that there is a local medical school that will want your body (see Chapter 13). As your will may not be read until after your funeral, it is of course sensible to let your family know your wishes. The law provides for you to make your wishes known either in writing or orally in the presence of two witnesses.

Here is a clause to put in your will.

> I wish to donate my body for anatomical examination after my death. If, in the course of the examinations, organs or tissue are removed, the medical school may retain or destroy them at its discretion. On completion of the anatomical examination, I wish my body to be *(buried/cremated)*.

Here is a form of authorisation for you to complete in your lifetime and give to your family. Keep a copy near your will.

ANATOMY ACT 1984

AUTHORISATION FOR USE OF MY BODY FOR ANATOMICAL EXAMINATION

TO MY EXECUTORS AND FAMILY

Full Name ....

Address ....

I wish to donate my body for anatomical examination after my death. If, in the course of the examinations, organs or tissue are removed, the medical school may retain or destroy them at its discretion. On completion of the anatomical examination, I wish my body to be *(buried/cremated)*.

Here are the details of the medical school which may be able to use my body: *(insert details here)*

Signature ....

Date: ....

Mutual wills

You may think that a **mutual will** is a neat way of making sure that your **assets** are not diverted by your spouse or partner after your death, such as to a new gold-digging lover, at the expense of your children. But think carefully, because there are severe practical problems. For example:

o   Do you intend the mutual wills to apply to assets that your spouse or partner acquires after your death?
o   What happens if your spouse or partner remarries? Remember, marriage revokes a will.
o   How is the agreement to be policed? Assets get bought and sold and mixed up with other assets; try unscrambling an omelette and you'll get some idea of the problems.
o   What about **lifetime gifts** by the survivor after you die?

Apart from all this, a mutual will seeks to impose a straitjacket on your spouse or partner after your death. Is this really a good thing?

Here is a clause declaring that you and your partner are making mutual wills.

Declaration that wills are mutual

My will is a mutual will with *(name of husband/wife/partner),* which he/she has signed at the same time that I have signed mine. We have agreed that neither of us during our joint lives or afterwards is to revoke (except by marriage) their will or to make any gift or settlement of any property or any further will or codicil which has a material adverse effect on any interest given by or under their will except during our joint lives by the written agreement of us both and after the death of one of us by the written agreement of each beneficiary whose interest is so affected. If either of us remarries they are to execute a further will containing such disposals as are necessary to give effect to the gifts made in our common wills. The new will does not need to apply to any property acquired by the survivor as a consequence of the remarriage but the survivor should keep such property separate from and not mixed with their other property.

And here is a declaration that two wills are *not* mutual:

Declaration

Although *(insert name)* is making a will in the same or similar form as I am, we agree that our wills are not binding on each other. We are each free to revoke our respective wills before or after the death of the other.

....

....

Signing, witnessing and safe keeping

Let us suppose you have taken all our advice and made your will. Congratulations – but it won't be legally binding until you sign it.

You need witnesses

Signing your will is one thing you *can't* do on your own. You need two adult, independent witnesses who are *not*:

o **beneficiaries** or their spouses or partners;

o members of your family;

o under 18 (under 16 in Scotland);

o blind;

o mentally incapable.

Until very recently, your executors and their spouses could not witness your will. They can now do so – provided they do not benefit under it. Our preference remains that executors and trustees, and their spouses and partners, should not act as witnesses because they are not fully independent.

Two neighbours or work colleagues would be ideal witnesses, as long as you don't plan to leave them anything in your will.

Remember, the **witnesses** are signing to say they have seen you sign your will. They do not need to know what is in your will.

How it's done

1. You sign your will first, in ink, at the very end of the will, with both witnesses watching. There is no need for them to read your will.
2. Both witnesses sign the will with you watching.
3. You date the will with the date of signing.
4. Both you and the witnesses should initial the bottom right hand corner of each page, except the page on which you sign.

Some don'ts

o Don't cheat! It could make the will invalid, and remember, a beneficiary who witnesses cannot inherit under your will.

o Don't staple or clip any other document to your will (but it's fine to put related documents in the same envelope).

o Don't cross anything out or make any alterations either before or after signing. They could make your will invalid.

o Don't try to add a PS after signing. It could make your will invalid.

o And don't try to make your will in anything other than in writing (video and audio wills are not yet acceptable!).

If you've slipped up – tear the whole thing up, download a fresh will form from our website and start again.

Hang on! What happens if ...

You cannot read your will, or write your signature?

As long as you have the mental capacity to do so, you can make a will regardless of your ability – physical or mental – to read or write. If you cannot read the will, it should be read over to you and you should confirm that you understand it before it is signed. If you are unable to write, the will can be signed by someone else on your behalf. The signature should be witnessed by two witnesses as before, and the signature clause should use a special form of words that describes what has been done. We provide this form of words on p 145.

Now – keep your will under review

A will 'speaks from death'. The will you make today may be out of date in no time at all. For example:

o   You marry, which has the effect of cancelling any existing will (unless you expressly state that it is written with your marriage in mind – see p 22).

o   You divorce, which will cancel any benefit for your former spouse.

o   You are in the throes of divorce proceedings, which will not cancel any benefit to your estranged spouse if you die before the decree absolute (see p 22).

o   A beneficiary dies before you – what will happen to their legacy?

o   Births, marriages and deaths – you want to benefit different people.

o   The assets you now own are much more, much less, or different than when you last made a will. Inheritance Tax may suddenly become important to you. Or you may not be able to be as generous as before. And remember that a gift of a specific asset will lapse if you do not own it when you die. It may seem a little heartless to leave someone an item you no longer own, but maybe that's what you want.

o   Changes in **Inheritance Tax** and/or Capital Gains Tax – if your will has been written with tax saving in mind, changes in tax law may blow your plans.

o   Accidental destruction – whoops! If you destroy your will on purpose, that will cancel it. If it is an accident – for example, the dog chews up the signed original of your will, there will, even if there is a copy in existence, be practical difficulties. Write and sign a new one.

Safe keeping

You need to keep your will somewhere sensible and easily accessible. You could ask your bank to take care of it, but they will charge you. And if you do choose to deposit your will with your bank, make sure your family know it is there.

For £15 you can take your will to your local Probate Registry (there is a complete list on the Court Service website at www. courtservice.gov.uk/cms/3798.htm) or post it to the Principal Registry (see 'Useful contacts'). They can keep your will safe and produce it for your executors on request. This is perhaps the safest bet of all.

But remember to tell your family where your will is – probate registrars don't scan the obituaries columns and contact the bereaved families on their own initiative! (See 'Make things easy for your executors', p 130.)

Sample wills

Administrative provisions

All the wills are available on our website. You can download as many as you want. Do have a 'dry run' before you invite your witnesses in!

Apart from saying who is to get what, a well-written will should tell your executors how to administer your estate. Most wills drown in oceans of verbiage to do this. We have cut all that out, but when necessary we have referred to the excellent provisions of the Society of Estate and Trust Practitioners. The Incorporated Provisions are the engine in the car: they are there for a reason, they work, but they do not need to be on display.

Which will is right for you?

These simple questions should help you to choose the right will for your needs.

Do you have a partner?

❑   Yes   Consider Wills 1, 3, 4, 8 and 9.

❑   No   Continue.

Do you want to leave everything to your partner?

❑   Yes   Will 1 is for you *if* – but only if – you do not have children or anyone else to consider, even a charity.

❑   No   Continue.

Do you have children?

❑   Yes   Consider Wills 2, 3, 8 and 9.

❑   No   Continue.

Do you have a child with a mental disability?

❑   Yes   Consider Will 7.

❑   No   Continue.

Do you want to leave everything to your partner, *but* if your partner dies first, everything to your children?

❑   Yes   You need Will 3. If you are worried about Inheritance Tax, consider also Wills 8 and 9.

❑   No   Continue.

Do you want to leave everything to your partner, *but* if your partner dies first, everything to a person or persons other than your children, or to charity?

❑   Yes   Consider Will 4.

❑   No   Continue.

Do you want to leave everything to charity?

❑   Yes   You need Will 5.

❑   No   Continue.

Do you want to do something which is not covered in this book?

❑   Yes   You need professional advice.

❑   No   Turn to the will that best suits your circumstances.

Will 1

This is the will to use if you want to leave everything to your husband, wife or partner (including your same-sex partner) and appoint them your sole executor.

Wills in which spouses or partners leave their entire estates to each other are often called **'mirror wills'**. This will is reproduced on the website and you can print off as many copies as you wish.

Points to consider

o **What is to happen if your spouse or partner dies before you?**

If you want to make a substitutional gift, then add the clause from 'Odds and Ends' on p 141. Otherwise, there will be an intestacy (see 'Buzzwords' and the 'Intestacy' diagram pp 4–5) on the second death.

o **What is to happen if your spouse or partner dies very shortly after you?**

The effect will be to 'bunch' your assets into your spouse's or partner's estate. This may not cause any problems unless:

– you and your spouse or partner would want to benefit different people after you are both dead;

– the joint estate is worth more than the nil rate band for **Inheritance Tax**. If it is, you may find that Inheritance Tax becomes payable on the second death: tax which is avoidable with careful planning.

One solution to these problems is to make the gift to your spouse or partner conditional on their surviving for, say, 30 days after you die (see Chapter 16).

o Consider also whether you should appoint a substitute executor in case your spouse or partner dies before you, or is unable to take the job on.

o Do you and your spouse/partner intend to write **mutual wills** (see p 148)?

Will of *[insert your full name]*

I *[insert your full name]*
of *[insert your full address]* revoke all earlier wills and declare this to be my last will ('my Will').

I give the whole of my estate to *[insert your spouse's or partner's full name]* and appoint *[insert your spouse's or partner's full name]* as my sole executor.

Funeral Arrangements

[Insert your preferred funeral arrangements here]

Dating, Signing and Witnessing

Date: ....

My signature ....

I have signed my Will to give it effect; *and*

I have done so in the presence of the two independent adult witnesses named below; *and*

Both witnesses have signed below in my presence; *and*

Neither of them can inherit under my Will; and (if applicable) neither can their husbands, wives or partners.

	Witness 1	Witness 2
Signature:	....	
Full name:	....	
Address:	....	
	....	
	....	
	....	
Occupation:	....	

Will 2

This is the will to use if you wish to leave everything to your children.

The will is reproduced on the website and you can print off as many copies as you wish.

Points to consider

o Is it possible that you might have more children before you die? Remember that both men and women can now produce children at advanced ages. Leave your options open in your will by referring to 'my children' rather than naming them individually.

o If you have children under 18, you may want to appoint **guardians**.

o If you have a child with special needs, consider Will 7.

o What is to happen if all your children die before you and they do not themselves leave any children? Consider a back-up option – a 'default **beneficiary**'.

o The gift to your children in this will is age-**contingent**. In the case of an outright gift to a child under 18, your will must provide for someone else to give the executors a receipt for the money, because the child cannot do so.

o In the form we use, all your children – legitimate, illegitimate or adopted – are equal under your will, *but* a child who you treat as your own, but of whom you are not the parent, such as a stepchild, will not benefit automatically. You should make special provision for such children, mentioning them by name.

Will of *[insert your full name]*

I *[insert your full name]*
of *[insert your full address]* revoke all earlier wills and declare this to be my last will ('my Will').

---

1 Executors and Trustees

1.1 I appoint as my executors *[insert full name]* of *[insert address]*

and *[insert full name]* of

[insert address].

1.2 In my Will the expression 'my Trustees' means the executors of my Will and the trustees of any trusts arising under it.

2 Guardians (only if you have children under 18)

I appoint *[insert full name]*

of *[insert address]*

and *[insert full name]*

of *[insert address]*

as guardians of any of my children who are under 18 when I die.

3 Trustees' Duties and Powers

3.1 My Trustees are to hold my estate on trust to retain or sell it and:

- pay my debts, the cost of my funeral and the expenses of administering my estate;
- pay any taxes arising from my death;
- distribute the gifts and give effect to the other beneficial intentions of my Will.

3.2 My Trustees are to have all the powers which the law and my Will confer for these purposes, and they are to exercise those powers with reasonable skill and care. If they need help, they are to seek professional advice and assistance.

4 Residuary Gift

Subject as above, I give my estate in equal shares to those of my children who survive me and attain the age of 18. But if any of my children dies before me, or before age 18, leaving children, then those children shall on attaining the age of 18 take equally the share which their parent would otherwise have taken.

5 Incorporated Provisions

The standard provisions of the Society of Trust and Estate Practitioners (1st edition) are to apply.

6 Funeral Arrangements

[Insert your preferred funeral arrangements here]

Dating, Signing and Witnessing

Date: ....

My signature ....

I have signed my Will to give it effect; *and*
I have done so in the presence of the two independent adult
witnesses named below; *and*
Both witnesses have signed below in my presence; *and*
Neither of them can inherit under my Will; and (if applicable)
neither can their husbands, wives or partners.

	Witness 1	Witness 2
Signature:	....	....
Full name:	....	....
Address:	....	....
	....	
	....	
	....	

Per stirpes

The above will spells out the **per stirpes** rule, which we mention in
the Buzzwords section. This rule applies automatically to gifts to your
own children (s 33 of the Wills Act 1837 refers) unless you specifically
say that this rule is not to apply. Its effect is as follows:

Suppose you have two children, Bill and Ben. You leave your estate
to them in equal shares when they reach the age of 18. Suppose Bill
dies *either*:

○ before you; *or*
○ before reaching the age of 18; *and*
○ leaves children

then those children will inherit Bill's share when they reach 18. If you
want to do something different (such as having Bill's share go to Ben
or indeed to Bill's wife Barbara), you have to say so explicitly,
preferably saying that s 33 of the Wills Act 1837 does not apply.

WILLS & ESTATE PLANNING

Will 3

This is the will to use if you want to leave everything to your spouse or partner, and if they die first, everything to your children.

In respect of the gift to your spouse or partner, see the comments on Will 1.

In respect of the gift to your children, see the comments on Will 2.

If you and your spouse or partner are not both the mother and the father of all the children (for example, if there are stepchildren), the form of will below may not benefit all the children you have in mind. Take professional advice.

The will is reproduced on the website and you can print off as many copies as you wish.

Will of *[insert your full name]*

I *[insert your full name]*
of *[insert your full address]* revoke all earlier wills and declare this to be my last will ('my Will').

Part 1

I give the whole of my estate to *[insert your spouse's or partner's full name]* and appoint *[insert your spouse's or partner's full name]* as my sole executor.

BUT if this gift fails then the provisions of Part 2 of my Will shall apply instead of Part 1.

Part 2

1 Executors and Trustees

1.1 I appoint as my executors *[insert full name]* of *[insert address]*
and *[insert full name]* of
[insert address].

1.2 In my Will the expression 'my Trustees' means the executors of my Will and the trustees of any trusts arising under it.

2 Guardians *(only if you have children under 18)*

I appoint *[insert full name]* of *[insert address]* and *[insert full name]* of *[insert address]* as guardians of any of my children who are under 18 when I die.

3 Trustees' Duties and Powers

3.1 My Trustees are to hold my estate on trust to retain or sell it and:

- pay my debts, the cost of my funeral and the expenses of administering my estate;
- pay any taxes arising from my death;
- distribute the gifts and give effect to the other beneficial intentions of my Will.

3.2 My Trustees are to have all the powers which the law and my Will confer for these purposes, and they are to exercise those powers with reasonable skill and care. If they need help, they are to seek professional advice and assistance.

4 Residuary Gift

Subject as above, I give my estate in equal shares to those of my children who survive me and attain the age of 18. But if any of my children dies before me, or before age 18, leaving children, then those children shall on attaining the age of 18 take equally the share which their parent would otherwise have taken.

Part 3

The provisions of Part 3 of my Will are of general application, and apply whether Part 1 or Part 2 applies.

Incorporated Provisions

The standard provisions of the Society of Trust and Estate Practitioners (1st edition) are to apply.

Funeral Arrangements

[Insert your preferred funeral arrangements here]

Dating, Signing and Witnessing

Date: ....

My signature ....

I have signed my Will to give it effect; *and*
I have done so in the presence of the two independent adult
witnesses named below; *and*
Both witnesses have signed below in my presence; *and*
Neither of them can inherit under my Will; and (if applicable)
neither can their husbands, wives or partners.

	Witness 1	Witness 2

Signature: ....

Full name: ....
Address: ....

....

....

....

Will 4

This is the will to use if you want to leave everything to your spouse or partner but, if your partner dies first, everything to other beneficiaries or to charity.

In respect of a gift to your spouse or partner, see the notes for Will 1.

In respect of gifts to charity, see p 36.

Gifts to charity are **exempt** from **Inheritance Tax**. Gifts to people, other than your spouse, are not exempt, although no tax may be payable as long as your estate does not exceed the **nil rate band**. There are potential tax problems if you divide your **residuary estate** between exempt and non-exempt **beneficiaries**. If you think this may apply to you, take professional advice.

The will is reproduced on the website and you can print off as many copies as you wish.

Will of *[insert your full name[*

I *[insert your full name]*
of *[insert your full address]* revoke all earlier wills and declare this to be my last will ('my Will').

Part 1

I give the whole of my estate to *[insert your spouse's or partner's full name]* and appoint *[insert your spouse's or partner's full name]* as my sole executor but if this gift fails then the provisions of Part 2 of my Will shall apply instead of Part 1.

Part 2

1 Executors and Trustees

1.1 I appoint as my executors *[insert full name]* of
[insert address]
and *[insert full name]* of
[insert address]

1.2 In my Will the expression 'my Trustees' means the executors of my Will and the trustees of any trusts arising under it.

2 Trustees' Duties and Powers

2.1 My Trustees are to hold my estate on trust to retain or sell it and:

- pay my debts, the cost of my funeral and the expenses of administering my estate;
- pay any taxes arising from my death;
- distribute the gifts and give effect to the other beneficial intentions of my Will.

2.2 My Trustees are to have all the powers which the law and my Will confer for these purposes, and they are to exercise those powers with reasonable skill and care. If they need help, they are to seek professional advice and assistance.

3 Residuary Gift

Subject as above, my Trustees are to divide and pay the residue of my estate as follows:

3.1 [   ] % to

[insert name and address of charity, and charity number]

3.2 [   ] % to *[insert name and address of charity, and charity number]*

3.3 [   ] % to *[insert name and address of charity, and charity number]*

3.4 [   ] % to *[insert name and address of charity, and charity number]*

Even if any charity named in my Will changes its name or constitution, or amalgamates with another charity, it is still to receive the benefit given by my Will.

If any charity named in my Will has ceased to exist, the benefit is to be given to another charity, selected by my Trustees, and having the same or similar charitable purposes.

Part 3

The provisions of Part 3 of my Will are of general application, and apply whether Part 1 or Part 2 applies.

Incorporated Provisions

The standard provisions of the Society of Trust and Estate Practitioners (1st edition) are to apply.

Funeral Arrangements

[Insert your preferred funeral arrangements here]

Dating, Signing and Witnessing

Date: ....

My signature ....

I have signed my Will to give it effect; *and*
I have done so in the presence of the two independent adult witnesses named below; *and*
Both witnesses have signed below in my presence; *and*
Neither of them can inherit under my Will; and (if applicable) neither can their husbands, wives or partners.

	Witness 1	Witness 2
Signature:	....	....
Full name:	....	....
Address:	....	....
	....	....
	....	....
	....	....
Occupation:	....	....

Will 5

This is the will to use if you want to leave everything to charity.

In respect of gifts to charity, see p 36.

The will is reproduced on the website and you can print off as many copies as you wish.

Will of *[insert your full name]*

I *[insert your full name]*

of *[insert your full address]* revoke all earlier wills and declare this to be my last will ('my Will').

1 Executors

I appoint as my executors *[insert full name]* of
[insert address]
and *[insert full name]* of
[insert address]

2 Executors' Duties and Powers

2.1 My Executors are to hold my estate on trust to retain or sell it and:

- pay my debts, the cost of my funeral and the expenses of administering my estate;
- pay any taxes arising from my death;
- distribute the gifts and give effect to the other beneficial intentions of my Will.

2.2 My Executors are to have all the powers which the law and my Will confer for these purposes, and they are to exercise those powers with reasonable skill and care. If they need help, they are to seek professional advice and assistance.

3 Residuary Gift

Subject as above, I give my estate as follows:

3.1 [ ] % to	*[insert name and address of charity and charity number]*
3.2 [ ] % to	*[insert name and address of charity and charity number]*
3.3 [ ] % to	*[insert name and address of charity and charity number]*
3.4 [ ] % to	*[insert name and address of charity and charity number]*

Even if any charity named in my Will changes its name or constitution, or amalgamates with another charity, it is still to receive the benefit given by my Will.

If any charity named in my Will has ceased to exist, the benefit is to be given to another charity, selected by my Trustees, and having the same or similar charitable purposes.

4 Incorporated Provisions

The standard provisions of the Society of Trust and Estate Practitioners (1st edition) are to apply.

5 Funeral Arrangements

[Insert your preferred funeral arrangements here]

Dating, Signing and Witnessing

Date: ....

My signature ....

I have signed my Will to give it effect; *and*
I have done so in the presence of the two independent adult witnesses named below; *and*
Both witnesses have signed below in my presence; *and*
Neither of them can inherit under my Will; and (if applicable) neither can their husbands, wives or partners.

	Witness 1	Witness 2
Signature:	....
Full name:	....
Address:	....
	....
Occupation:	....

Will 6

This will gives everything to named beneficiaries other than charities.

The main issue with this type of will is: what happens if a named beneficiary dies before you? In our form of will, we provide that the deceased beneficiary's share is divided *pro rata* between the surviving beneficiaries. An alternative would be for the deceased beneficiary's share to go to their spouse, partner or children.

Will of *[insert your full name]*

I *[insert your full name]*
of *[insert your full address]* revoke all earlier wills and declare this to be my last will ('my Will').

1 Executors and Trustees

1.1 I appoint as my executors *[insert full name]* of
[insert address]
and *[insert full name]* of
[insert address].

1.2 In my Will the expression 'my Trustees' means the executors of my Will and the trustees of any trusts arising under it.

2 Trustees' Duties and Powers

2.1 My Trustees are to hold my estate on trust to retain or sell it and:

- pay my debts, the cost of my funeral and the expenses of administering my estate;
- distribute the gifts and give effect to the other beneficial intentions of my Will.

2.2 My Trustees are to have all the powers which the law and my Will confer for these purposes, and they are to exercise those powers with reasonable skill and care. If they need help, they are to seek professional advice and assistance.

3 Residuary Gift

Subject as above, my Trustees are to divide and pay the residue of my estate as follows:

3.1 [   ] % to   *[insert name and address of beneficiary]*
3.2 [   ] % to   *[insert name and address of beneficiary]*
3.3 [   ] % to   *[insert name and address of beneficiary]*
3.4 [   ] % to   *[insert name and address of beneficiary]*

If any beneficiary named in my will dies before me, the deceased beneficiary's share is to be added pro rata to the shares of the other beneficiaries.

4 Incorporated Provisions

The standard provisions of the Society of Trust and Estate Practitioners (1st edition) are to apply.

5 Funeral Arrangements

[Insert your preferred funeral arrangements here]

Dating, Signing and Witnessing

Date: ....

My signature   ....

I have signed my Will to give it effect; *and*
I have done so in the presence of the two independent adult witnesses named below; *and*
Both witnesses have signed below in my presence; *and*
Neither of them can inherit under my Will; and (if applicable) neither can their husbands, wives or partners.

	Witness 1	Witness 2
Signature:	....	....
Full name:	....	....
Address:	....	....
	....	....
Occupation:	....	....

Will 7

This will provides a **discretionary trust** for a child of any age with a mental disability. The distinguishing feature of a discretionary trust is that there is no one who can claim a right to the money, and the purpose of this is to protect the child's right to state benefits. Because the trust is discretionary, there have to be other potential **beneficiaries** – otherwise it creates what is known as an 'interest in possession in the money' (see 'Interest in possession trust', p 93). One consequence of this is that unscrupulous **trustees** could divert the money away from the child with the disability towards other potential beneficiaries. You must therefore be able to trust your trustees!

Before the trustees spend money for the disabled child's benefit, they should always see what other sources of funding (for example, grants) may be available.

A discretionary trust for a disabled person can confer important **Inheritance Tax** and Capital Gains Tax advantages – as long as the trust complies with strict rules.

Inheritance Tax

Here are the rules:

o   The disabled person must be someone who is:
  –   incapable as a result of mental disorder of managing their own affairs; or
  –   receiving Attendance Allowance; or
  –   receiving Disability Living Allowance.
o   During the life of the disabled person, the trust must be a discretionary trust.
o   The terms of the trust must ensure that if capital is used during the life of the disabled person, not less than half of the capital which is actually spent, is spent for the disabled person's benefit.

A trust which complies with these rules escapes Inheritance Tax on capital payments to the disabled person and the usual 10-yearly charge which applies to discretionary trusts. Moreover, lifetime gifts into the trust are treated as **PETs** (if it wasn't for this exemption, such gifts might attract Inheritance Tax at the lifetime rate (20%)).

Capital Gains Tax

Here are the rules:

o   As before, the trust must be for the benefit of a disabled person (see above).

o   As before, the terms of the trust must ensure that if capital is used during the life of the disabled person, not less than half of the capital which is actually spent, is spent for the disabled person's benefit.

o   The disabled person must be entitled to not less than half of the income of the trust fund, *or* no such income may be applied for the benefit of anyone else.

Where a trust complies with these rules, the trustees are entitled to the individual's annual exemption, which in the tax year 2004/05 is £8,200 instead of the trustee's exemption, which is half that amount.

The **Inheritance Tax** concession applies where there is a discretionary trust, although to qualify for the Capital Gains Tax concession the disabled person must be 'entitled to not less than half of the income'. *But* if the disabled person is entitled to the income, the trust is not discretionary. Catch 22? Will 7 gets round this problem, at least as far as is possible.

There is little readily accessible official guidance on trusts for disabled people. There is some information on the Inland Revenue website: find your way to Help Sheets IR294 and IHT16. Mencap offers a booklet – click on www.mencap.org.uk. There is also useful advice at www.housingoptions.org.uk/factsheets/19-discretionary.htm.

You will see that the tax advantages are also available for a beneficiary who has a physical disability and receives associated benefits, typically Disability Living Allowance.

Bear in mind that some Inheritance Tax will be payable if your gift to your child with special needs exceeds *either:*

- the nil rate band (£263,000 in the tax year 2004/05);
  or

- what is left of your **nil rate band** after taking into account **lifetime gifts** which have not timed out by the time you die.

The alternative might be a gift to a charity which specialises in the care of people with the same disability as your child. The tax advantage is that charities are exempt beneficiaries and no Inheritance Tax would be payable on your gift (see Chapter 6, 'Special beneficiaries'). The disadvantage in human terms is that you cannot be sure the money will benefit your child directly.

Will of *[insert your full name]*

I *[insert your full name]*
of *[insert your full address]* revoke all earlier wills and declare this to be my last will ('my Will').

1 Executors and Trustees

1.1 I appoint as my executors *[insert full name]* of
[insert address]
and *[insert full name]* of
[insert address] .
1.2 In my Will the expression 'my Trustees' means the executors of my Will and the trustees of any trusts arising under it.

2 Guardians *(only if you have children under 18)*

I appoint *[insert full name]* of
[insert address]   and   *[insert full name]*   of
[insert address] as guardians of any of my children who are under 18 when I die.

3 Trustees' Duties and Powers

3.1 My Trustees are to hold my estate on trust to retain or sell it and:
- pay my debts, the cost of my funeral and the expenses of administering my estate;

- pay any taxes arising from my death;
- distribute the gifts and give effect to the other beneficial intentions of my Will.

3.2 My Trustees are to have all the powers which the law and my Will confer for these purposes, and they are to exercise those powers with reasonable skill and care. If they need help, they are to seek professional advice and assistance.

4 Discretionary Legacy for Children, Including a Child with a Disability

4.1 In this legacy and the gift of residue:

'My child with special needs' means *[insert name of disabled child]*

'The trust gift' means: £

'The trust fund' means: the assets which my trustees hold on the terms of trust set out in this clause. The trust gift is the initial capital of the trust fund.

'The trust beneficiaries' means:
- my child with special needs;
- my other children;
- my grandchildren born before the death of my child with special needs.

4.2 If my child with special needs survives me, I give the trust gift free of taxes to my trustees on the terms set out in this legacy.

4.3 During the lifetime of my child with special needs my Trustees are at their discretion to:

- use all or part of the income from the trust fund for the benefit of my child with special needs, and for not more than 21 years to save any remaining income;
- apply the capital of the trust fund for the benefit of the trust beneficiaries, but not less than half of the capital which the trustees so apply must be applied for the benefit of my child with special needs.

4.4 As well as their implied powers, my trustees have the discretionary power to use all or any part of the capital and/or income of the trust fund for the benefit of my child with special needs to pay the cost of:

- altering or adapting any living accommodation, whoever owns it, for the convenience and comfort of my child with special needs;
- providing domestic appliances and/or domestic help for my child with special needs and/or for whoever is living with or caring for them at that time;

- providing vehicles appropriate to the needs of my child with special needs and/or for whoever is living with or caring for them at that time;
- providing holidays for my child with special needs and/or anyone living with or caring for them at that time.

4.5 My trustees can also use all or part of the income or capital of the trust fund to buy a financial product (such as an annuity) to provide financial security for my child with special needs, even though this may use the whole of the trust fund.

4.6 My trustees can allow any dwelling forming part of the trust fund to be used as a home for my child with special needs, either alone or with someone else. In the latter case, my trustees need not make the other person pay rent, so long as the arrangement benefits my child with special needs.

4.7 Upon the death of my child with special needs, my trustees can use money from the trust fund to pay the funeral expenses and also, at their discretion, the cost of a memorial.

4.8 After the death of my child with special needs, my trustees are to use the income and capital of the trust fund for the benefit of the other trust beneficiaries and within one year my trustees are to distribute what remains of the trust fund to whichever of the other trust beneficiaries they choose. In making this final distribution, my trustees need not ensure equality between the other trust beneficiaries, or benefit all of them.

5 Residuary Gift to Children Other Than My Child with Special Needs

Subject as above, my trustees are to divide my estate equally among those of my children, other than my child with special needs, who survive me and attain the age of 18. If any of my children dies before me, or before age 18, leaving children, then those children shall on attaining the age of 18 take equally the share which their parent would otherwise have taken.

6 Incorporated Provisions

The standard provisions of the Society of Trust and Estate Practitioners (1st edition) are to apply.

7 Funeral Arrangements

[Insert your preferred funeral arrangements here]

Dating, Signing and Witnessing

Date: ....

My signature ....

I have signed my Will to give it effect; *and*
I have done so in the presence of the two independent adult
witnesses named below; *and*
Both witnesses have signed below in my presence; *and*
Neither of them can inherit under my Will; and (if applicable)
neither can their husbands, wives or partners.

	Witness 1	Witness 2

Signature: ....

Full name: ....
Address: ....
....
....
....

Occupation: ....

Will 8

This will enables you to make a **nil rate band** gift to your children, with the balance of your estate going to your spouse. For **Inheritance Tax** purposes, the purpose of the will is to take maximum advantage of the nil rate band, that is, to give as much as you can to non-**exempt beneficiaries** – your children – when you die, without paying Inheritance Tax. The residue of your estate goes to your spouse. There will be no tax to pay as long as your spouse outlives you because your spouse is an exempt beneficiary. At the time of writing, the gift of residue will not be exempt from Inheritance Tax if you and your partner are not married. For further discussion of nil rate band gifts, see Strategy 7, p 67.

If a nil rate band gift to your children might leave your widow or widower short of money, consider a nil rate band **discretionary trust** – see Will 9 below.

Note that you will need to revise your will if the Inheritance Tax rules change or if Inheritance Tax is replaced by some other tax.

Will of *[insert your full name]*

I *[insert your full name]*
of *[insert your full address]* revoke all earlier wills and declare this to be my last will ('my Will').

1 Appointment of Executors

I appoint as my executors *[insert full name]* of *[insert address]*
and *[insert full name]* of
[insert address].

2 Trustees' Duties and Powers

2.1 My Trustees are to hold my estate on trust to retain or sell it and:

- pay my debts, the cost of my funeral and the expenses of administering my estate;

- pay any taxes arising from my death;

- distribute the gifts and give effect to the other beneficial intentions of my Will.

2.2 My Trustees are to have all the powers which the law and my Will confer for these purposes, and they are to exercise those powers with reasonable skill and care. If they need help, they are to seek professional advice and assistance.

3 Nil Rate Band Gift to Children

3.1 In this clause 3, 'the nil rate band gift' means the maximum amount which I can give to my children under this clause without Inheritance Tax becoming payable either on:

- the nil rate band gift; *and/or*
- lifetime gifts made by me on which Inheritance Tax will become payable as a result of my death.

The nil rate band gift is to exclude:

- assets which are exempt from Inheritance Tax; *and*
- assets to which reliefs apply, such as business property relief and/or agricultural property relief.

3.2 If, but only if, *[insert name of spouse]* survives me, I give the nil rate band gift free of taxes in equal shares to my children on attaining the age of 18. But if any of my children dies before me, or before the age of 18, leaving children, then those children shall on attaining the age of 18 take equally the share which their parent would otherwise have taken.

4 Residuary Gift

4.1 Subject as above, I give the residue of my estate to *[insert name of spouse]*.

4.2 If *[insert name of spouse]* does not survive me, I give the residue of my estate in equal shares to my children on attaining the age of 18. But if any of my children dies before me, or before the age of 18, leaving children, then those children shall on attaining the age of 18 take equally the share which their parent would otherwise have taken.

5 Incorporated Provisions

The standard provisions of the Society of Trust and Estate Practitioners (1st edition) are to apply.

6 Funeral Arrangements

[Insert your preferred funeral arrangements here]

Dating, Signing and Witnessing

Date: ....

My signature ....

I have signed my Will to give it effect; *and*
I have done so in the presence of the two independent adult
witnesses named below; *and*
Both witnesses have signed below in my presence; *and*
Neither of them can inherit under my Will; and (if applicable)
neither can their husbands, wives or partners.

	Witness 1	Witness 2

Signature: ....

Full name: ....
Address: ....

....

....

....

Occupation: ....

Will 9

This will sets up a **nil rate band discretionary trust** for your spouse, children and grandchildren, with the balance of your estate going to your spouse. For **Inheritance Tax** tax purposes, the purpose of the will is to take maximum advantage of the nil rate band – that is, to give as much as you can to non-exempt beneficiaries when you die – without paying Inheritance Tax. You can achieve the same tax advantage by making an outright gift to the non-**exempt beneficiaries**. But will your widower or widower have enough money to live on if you make an outright gift to, say, your children? A discretionary trust lets you have it both ways, because you can include your widow or widower as a potential beneficiary of the trust. So the money in the trust can still benefit your widow or widower but will stay out of their estate. You therefore avoid the 'bunching' of assets on the second death. For further discussion of nil rate band discretionary trusts, see Strategy 8, p 67.

This will can be adapted to provide a two-year discretionary trust – see p 96.

Where you set up a discretionary trust, it is often sensible to write a separate 'letter of wishes' which expresses the way you hope your trustees will use the fund. Note, however, that the letter of wishes will not be binding on your trustees – because otherwise the trust would not be discretionary!

Note that you will need to revise your will if the Inheritance Tax rules change or if Inheritance Tax is replaced by some other tax.

Will of *[insert your full name]*

I *[insert your full name]*

of *[insert your full address]* revoke all earlier wills and declare this to be my last will ('my Will').

---

1 Appointment of Executors

I appoint as my executors *[insert full name]* of
[insert address]
and *[insert full name]* of
[insert address] .

2 Executors' Duties and Powers

2.1 My Executors are to hold my estate on trust to retain or sell it and:

- pay my debts, the cost of my funeral and the expenses of administering my estate;
- pay any taxes arising from my death;
- distribute the gifts and give effect to the other beneficial intentions of my Will.

2.2 My Executors are to have all the powers which the law and my Will confer for these purposes, and they are to exercise those powers with reasonable skill and care. If they need help, they are to seek professional advice and assistance.

3 Nil Rate Band Discretionary Trust

3.1 In this clause 3:

- 'My trustees' means *[insert names of trustees – there must be not less than two, and they can be the same people as your executors]*.
- 'The trust gift' means the maximum amount which I can give to my trustees under this clause without Inheritance Tax becoming payable either on:
  - the trust gift; *and/or*
  - lifetime gifts made by me on which Inheritance Tax will become payable as a result of my death.

  The trust gift is to exclude:
  - assets which are exempt from Inheritance Tax; *and*
  - assets to which reliefs apply, such as business property relief and/or agricultural property relief.
- 'The fund' means the assets held by my trustees on the trust declared in this clause 3, including any additions to it after my death.
- 'My beneficiaries' are:
  - *[insert name of spouse]*
  - my children;

- my grandchildren born no later than the end of the distribution period.

- 'The distribution period' means the period starting not earlier than three months after my death and ending not later than 80 years after my death.

3.2 If, but only if, *[insert name of spouse]* survives me, I give the trust gift to my trustees free of taxes to hold under the terms of the trust set out in clause 3.3.

3.3 My trustees are, during the distribution period, to:

- apply the income of the fund for the benefit of such of my beneficiaries as my trustees think fit, or (for not more than 21 years from my death) to save the whole or any part of the income;

- apply the capital of the fund for the benefit of such of my beneficiaries as my trustees think fit; and

- wind up the trust before the last day of the distribution period by distributing the fund among such of my beneficiaries as my trustees think fit.

3.4 My trustees may exercise their discretionary powers when and how they think fit, and need not make any payments to or for the benefit of all my beneficiaries, nor ensure equality among those whom they do benefit. My trustees have the power to take account of unborn potential beneficiaries, but they do not have a duty to do so.

3.5 If my trustees fail to exercise their discretion to distribute the fund before the last day of the distribution period, then on that date my trustees are to distribute the fund equally among those of my beneficiaries who are then alive.

4 Residuary Gift

4.1 Subject as above, I give the residue of my estate to *[insert name of spouse]*.

4.2 If *[insert name of spouse]* does not survive me, my executors are to divide the residue of my estate equally among those of my children who are alive at the time of my death and attain the age of 18. But of any of my children dies before me, or before age 18, leaving children, then those children shall on attaining the age of 18 take equally the share which their parent would otherwise have taken.

5 Incorporated Provisions

The standard provisions of the Society of Trust and Estate Practitioners (1st edition) are to apply.

6 Funeral Arrangements

[Insert your preferred funeral arrangements here]

Dating, Signing and Witnessing

Date: ....

My signature ....

I have signed my Will to give it effect; *and*
I have done so in the presence of the two independent adult witnesses named below; *and*
Both witnesses have signed below in my presence; *and*
Neither of them can inherit under my Will; and (if applicable) neither can their husbands, wives or partners.

	Witness 1	Witness 2
Signature:	....	
Full name:	....	
Address:	....	
	....	
	....	
	....	
Occupation:	....	

Deed of variation

Most people think of wills as written in stone. This need not be the case. We have mentioned that your **beneficiaries** can, in certain circumstances, change your will after your death, and there may be tax advantages in doing so (see Strategy 10, p 70). If your beneficiaries want to vary your will, they need a deed of variation. There are strict rules which they must follow in order to get the tax advantages. We explain these rules in Strategy 10. Here is a sample. You will, of course, change the names!

Note that while you need two **witnesses** for a will, only one is required for a deed of variation.

Deed of Variation

This deed is made on 30 August 2004

By me, Betty Grench of Turtle Drive, Giggleswick.

Definitions

'Ferdinand' – my husband, Ferdinand Grench, who expired in a fit of indignation on 1 July 2004.

'Ferdinand's Will' – Ferdinand's will, dated 1 April 2001 and for which probate was granted on 25 August 2004.

Background

Under Ferdinand's will he appointed me his sole executor, gave £1,000 to the Society for the Preservation of Windfarms (Charity No 104, 'The Rats' Nest', Lynchpin Close, Doncaster DN1 4PR) and left the residue of his estate to me.

I wish to vary Ferdinand's will to give a nil rate band legacy to my beloved only son Algernon Grench.

Operative Provisions

1 Ferdinand's will is to be varied by inserting a new clause as follows:

I give £263,000 free of taxes to my son Algernon Grench.

2 I intend that Section 142(1) Inheritance Tax Act 1984 and Secion 62(6) Taxation of Chargeable Gains Act 1992 shall apply to this deed.

---

3 It is hereby certified that this deed falls within category L in the Schedule to the Stamp Duty (Exempt Instruments) Regulations 1987.

Signed as a deed by me,
Betty Grench

in the presence of

Witness signature

Witness name

Witness address

Witness Occupation

Useful contacts

Organ donation

Organ Donationline
Tel: 0845 606 0400
open 7 am to 11 pm, seven days a week

The NHS Organ Donor Register
PO Box 14
FREEPOST
Patchway
Bristol
BS34 8ZZ

www.gift-of-life.org.uk/donor_register or
www.uktransplant.org.uk/odronline/servlet/mydetails
servlet to register online.

We also liked *Become an Organ Donor – so life can go on*, at
www.elmbridge.gov.uk/council/information/organdonor.
htm

Whole body donation

HM Inspector of Anatomy
Department of Health
Room 611
Wellington House
135–53 Waterloo Road
London SE1 8UG

Tel: 020 7972 4551/4342
Fax: 020 7972 4791

London Anatomy Office
Tel: 020 8846 1216

Department of Health

Alexander Fleming House
Elephant and Castle
London SE1 6BY

www.dh.gov.uk

Tissue donation – drug research

Department of Histology

Peterborough District Hospital
Thorpe Road
Peterborough PE3 6DA

Tel: 01733 874 000

Court of Protection (for enduring powers of attorney)

Customer Services Unit (Mental Health)

Public Guardianship Office
Protection Division
Stewart House
24 Kingsway
London WC2B 6JX

Tel: 020 7664 7000

Safe keeping for your will

Principal Registry

First Avenue House
42–49 High Holborn
London WC1V 6NP

Tel: 020 7947 6000

www.courtservice.gov.uk

Leaving money to charity

You can find out more in a helpful leaflet, *Leave the World a Better Place*. The leaflet is intended for solicitors but is admirably jargon-free. It is available on the web at www.rememberacharity.org.uk

Charities Digest

Published annually by Waterlow Information Services Limited; ISBN 1 85783 803 3, for a list of the main charities in the UK

MENCAP

National Centre
123 Golden Lane
London EC1Y 0RT

Tel: 020 7454 0454

www.mencap.org.uk

Mencap Trust Company Limited

Tel: 020 7696 6932

email: legacies@mencap.org.uk
www.mencap.org.uk/html/fundraising/leaving_a_legacy.htm

Charity Commissioners

Tel: 0870 333 0123 for the central register
Web: www.charity-commission.gov.uk
You can search for charities by name or by type of charity

Charities Aid Foundation

Trust Department
Kings Hill
West Malling
Kent ME19 4TA

Tel : 01732 520 000

www.cafonline.org

National Schizophrenia Fellowship

NSF Trustees Limited
28 Castle Street
Kingston-upon-Thames
Surrey KT1 1SS

Tel: 0208 547 3937

Guardians

Child Benefit

You can get a claim pack by calling 0845 302 1444 or download one from www.dwp.gov.uk

Guardian's Allowance

To get a claim pack, call the Guardian's Allowance Unit on 0845 302 1464. Alternatively, you can download a Guardian's Allowance booklet and form. Go to:

www.dwp.gov.uk/lifeevent/benefits/
guardians_allowance.asp

Child Support Agency National Helpline

Tel: 08457 133 133

www.csa.gov.uk

The family home

HM Land Registry

www.landreg.gov.uk

Inland Revenue

Website: www.inlandrevenue.gov.uk
For Inheritance Tax matters, go to www.inlandrevenue. gov.uk/leaflets/iht.htm. The ones we found most helpful were: IHT3 Inheritance Tax, An Introduction, IHT2 Inheritance Tax on Lifetime Gifts and IHT17 Businesses, Farms and Woodlands.

Financial advisers

Financial Services Authority
Tel: 020 7066 1000
Helpline: 0845 606 1234

Website: www.fsa.gov.uk

SOFA – the Society of Financial Advisers
www.sofa.org

Tel: 020 7417 4442

IFA Promotion: 0800 085 5000
www.unbiased.co.uk

Funerals, etc

British Humanist Association
1 Gower Street
London WC1E 6HD

Tel: 020 7079 3580
Fax: 020 7079 3588

www.humanism.org.uk

The BHA offers advice on non-religious funerals – check out their free factsheet: download it from www.humanism.org.uk. It also publishes the booklet *Funerals Without God* at £4.50.

Natural Death Centre
6 Blackstock Mews
Blackstock Road
London N4 2BT

Tel: 0871 288 2098
Fax: 020 7354 3831
email: ndc@alberyfoundation.org
www.naturaldeath.org.uk

The Natural Death Centre offers advice on green burials, DIY funerals and many other things. They also edit *The Natural Death Handbook,* edited by Nicholas Albery and Stephanie Wienrich, published by Rider at £10.99 (£14.99 by mail order from the Natural Death Centre).

Lesbian and Gay Christian Movement

For advice on Christian funerals for gay people, including details of sympathetic clergy near you (not all priests or pastors are willing to conduct funerals for gay people).

Tel: 020 7739 1249

www.lgcm.org.uk

National Association of Funeral Directors

618 Warwick Road
Solihull
West Midlands B91 1AA

Tel: 0845 230 1343

email: info@nafd.org.uk
www.nafd.org.uk

National Society of Allied and Independent Funeral Directors

3 Bullfields
Sawbridgeworth
Herts CM21 9DB

www.saif.org.uk

Muslim funerals

Mr Ebrahim Ahmed Jaset
Secretary
Muslim Burial Council of Leicestershire
394 East Park Road
Leicester LE5 5HL

Tel/Fax: 0116 273 0141

email: admin@mbcol.org.uk

Office of Fair Trading

Consumer guidance on funerals
www.oft.gov.uk/Consumer/Your+Rights+When+
Shopping/Funerals

Cremation Society of Great Britain

Brecon House (2nd floor)
16/16a Albion Place
Maidstone
Kent ME14 5DZ

Tel: 01622 688 292/3

Fax: 01622 686 698

email: cremsoc@aol.com

Website: www.cremation.org.uk

Index

WILLS & ESTATE PLANNING

Notes

Notes

Notes

Notes

Notes

Notes

Notes

Notes

Notes

Notes

Notes

The *Pocket Lawyer* series

To order any of the titles in the *Pocket Lawyer* series, contact

Cavendish Publishing Limited
The Glass House
Wharton Street
London WC1X 9PX

email: info@cavendishpublishing.com

web: www.cavendishpublishing.com

Tel: 020 7278 8000

Fax: 020 7278 8080